PUFF

Fantastic Mr Dahl

MICHAEL ROSEN was brought up in London. He originally tried to study medicine before starting to write stories and poems. His first book for children, *Mind Your Own Business*, illustrated by Quentin Blake, was published in 1974 and since then he has written many award-winning picture books and poetry collections. Michael spends all of his time writing books and articles for newspapers and magazines, visiting schools and libraries and performing his poetry, making radio programmes about words and language, and teaching at universities on reading and writing. Michael has received many honours and was made the fifth Children's Laureate in 2007–2009.

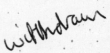

Fantastic Mr Dahl

MICHAEL ROSEN

PUFFIN

PUFFIN BOOKS

Published by the Penguin Group
Penguin Books Ltd, 80 Strand, London WC2R 0RL, England
Penguin Group (USA) Inc., 375 Hudson Street, New York, New York 10014, USA
Penguin Group (Canada), 90 Eglinton Avenue East, Suite 700, Toronto, Ontario, Canada M4P 2Y3
(a division of Pearson Penguin Canada Inc.)
Penguin Ireland, 25 St Stephen's Green, Dublin 2, Ireland (a division of Penguin Books Ltd)
Penguin Group (Australia), 250 Camberwell Road, Camberwell, Victoria 3124, Australia
(a division of Pearson Australia Group Pty Ltd)
Penguin Books India Pvt Ltd, 11 Community Centre, Panchsheel Park, New Delhi – 110 017, India
Penguin Group (NZ), 67 Apollo Drive, Rosedale, Auckland 0632, New Zealand
(a division of Pearson New Zealand Ltd)
Penguin Books (South Africa) (Pty) Ltd, Block D, Rosebank Office Park, 181 Jan Smuts Avenue,
Parktown North, Gauteng 2193, South Africa

Penguin Books Ltd, Registered Offices: 80 Strand, London WC2R 0RL, England

puffinbooks.com

First published 2012

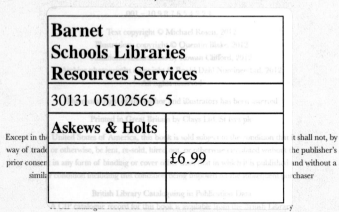

001–10 9 8 7 6 5 4 3 2 1

Text copyright © Michael Rosen, 2012

Illustrations copyright © Quentin Blake, 2012

Illustrations copyright © Rowan Clifford, 2012

Illustrations copyright © David Nuttall and Dad Numbers Ltd, 2012

The moral right of the author and illustrators has been asserted

Printed in Great Britain by Clays Ltd, St Ives plc

British Library Cataloguing in Publication Data
A CIP catalogue record for this book is available from the British Library

ISBN: 978-0-141-32213-1

www.greenpenguin.co.uk

MIX
Paper from
responsible sources
FSC
www.fsc.org   FSC™ C018179

Penguin Books is committed to a sustainable
future for our business, our readers and our
planet. This book is made from paper certified
by the Forest Stewardship Council.

Roald Dahl's motto

My candle burns at both ends;
It will not last the night;
But ah, my foes, and oh, my friends —
It gives a lovely light!
— Edna St Vincent Millay

Contents

Introduction   1

The Boy

1   Homesick   9
2   School Days   23
3   Letters   39
4   Holidays   61
5   Teenage Years   73

The Man

6   Travels   91
7   War Hero and Spy   105

The Writer

8   Gremlins   113
9   Family   123
10   How He Wrote the Books   135

Postscript   157

Acknowledgements   160
Bibliography   159

For Emma, Elsie and Emile
and for Joe, who was there for
Roald to talk to

Introduction

I first met Roald Dahl in a television studio in 1980. He was already very famous, though perhaps not quite as mega-famous as he is today. He'd written *James and the Giant Peach*, *Charlie and the Chocolate Factory*, *Fantastic Mr Fox* and *Danny the Champion of the World*. But now he had a new book out. And so did I. We were both appearing in the same TV programme because someone thought that we were writing similar kinds of stories. To tell the truth, I was quite excited. I was going to meet a writer whose books millions of children loved. But there was someone else with me who was even more excited than I was. This was my son Joe, who was about five years old.

In TV studios, there's often a little room away from all the cameras, where you wait until it's your turn to be filmed. It's called the green room – even though it's not usually green. Joe and I sat on one side of this particular green room and Roald Dahl was on the other. I noticed that he didn't really look at me even though I looked at him and tried to say hello. Instead, every now and then, Roald Dahl looked across at Joe. This went on for some time. After a bit, Roald caught Joe's attention and said to him in quite a stern way, 'Come here.'

Joe looked at me and I nodded. So he went over and stood in front of Roald Dahl. And, as everyone will tell you, Roald was very big – even when he was sitting down. Big legs, big body, even a big head. For a little boy, he must have seemed huge. A real giant.

Then, in a big, booming voice, Roald Dahl said to Joe, 'What's that growing on your father's face?'

Joe looked across the room at me and then back at Roald Dahl. In a small voice, he said, 'A beard?'

'Exactly!' said Roald Dahl. 'And it's disgusting!'

Joe looked unsure. Was this a joke or was it serious? He smiled, but only a little.

Roald Dahl went on, 'It's probably got this morning's breakfast in it. And last night's dinner. And old bits of rubbish, any old stuff that he's come across. You might even find a bicycle wheel in it.'

Joe looked back again at me and my beard. I could see on his face that there was a part of him that believed what he had just heard. After all, Roald Dahl hadn't asked Joe what he thought *might* be in my beard. He'd just told him in that firm, very sure voice what was actually, really and very definitely in my beard.

And that's what Roald Dahl was like. When he spoke, he did sound very, very certain – even if what he was saying was extraordinary, amazing, weird, fantastical or downright crazy.

Soon after that, Roald and I were called into the studio – me to talk about my book about a giant flea that lived in the London Underground and Roald Dahl to talk about . . . can you guess? *The Twits,* of course.

It's all a long time ago now, but I seem to remember that the interviewer asked us what we thought were the 'ingredients' of a good story for children.

'Above all,' Roald Dahl told the interviewer, 'it must be FUNNY.'

Afterwards, we returned to the green room, picked up our coats and went home. I think he said goodbye to me. He certainly said goodbye to little Joe, and had a few words of wisdom for him too. He leaned towards my son and said, 'And don't forget what I said about your father's beard.'

This book is about one of the world's greatest storytellers. Roald Dahl tells the story of his life in *Boy* and *Going Solo*. And, like Roald Dahl did, I want to tell you about things that happened to him that were deeply interesting and, more often than not, utterly, utterly amazing. But, most of all, I want to look closely at his writing.

I'm a writer and when I meet children, they often ask me how I got into writing. Why did I start? Where do I get my ideas from? Where do I write? How long does it take me to finish a book or a poem? What's my next book about?

In this book, I'm going to try to answer these questions about Roald Dahl's writing, along with one more. A little like the TV interviewer, I'd like to discover the special ingredients that, when mixed together, made Roald Dahl such an amazing a writer of children's books.

Now, a warning: it's impossible to write the whole, true story of anything. We always leave things out. We quite often put things in. Sometimes, no matter how hard we try not to, we change things. We tell the story in our own way, which might not be the same way that someone else would tell it. This book is my point of view. I'm looking at all the things I've read and heard about Roald Dahl, and choosing some of them to tell you about, in my particular way.

Writing often looks simple, clear and truthful, but it's always more complicated than it seems. This book is about that. It's about writing.

Duckworth Butterflies – Roald Dahl's house at St Peter's

Roald Dahl in his St Peter's school uniform

The Boy

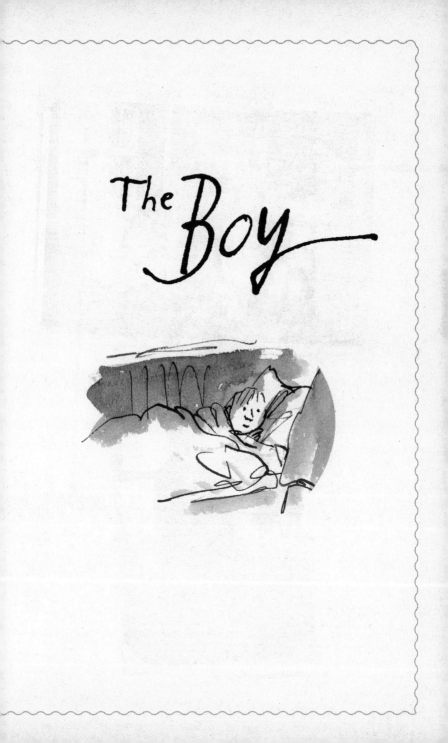

Else, Roald and Alfhild

Chapter 1

Homesick

To understand how Roald Dahl became such a fantastic writer, I think it's important to find out what he was like as a boy. Let's picture him, aged about nine years old when he first went to boarding school.

It was called St Peter's, and it was a long way from home, near the seaside town of Weston-super-Mare in Somerset, England. There were about seventy boys there, aged between eight and thirteen. No girls. St Peter's didn't really look like a school. It was more like the kind of spooky house you find in ghost stories, with dark, pointed windows and ivy creeping all over the outside walls.

The boys were grouped into 'houses', which meant that they lived together in different parts of the school. Each house had a name: Duckworth Butterflies, Duckworth Grasshoppers, Crawford Butterflies and Crawford Grasshoppers. And Roald was a Duckworth Butterfly. The four houses were like teams. They competed against each other in sports, schoolwork and almost everything. So, really, Roald belonged not just to a school but to a house within that school.

Most of Roald's teachers had fought in the First World War, which would have been a terrible, terrifying, scary time for them. They would nearly all have seen and heard awful, frightening things; they would all have been saddened by knowing someone who had been killed. Some of them would have been badly injured. In one of his letters home, Roald told his mother about a new teacher:

'Mr Jopp, he has only got one hand, he was in the air force.'

Some of these teachers were fierce. Some of them did odd, crazy things, like chasing the boys around on school trolleys! Many of them were keen on teaching the boys to love the finest things in life, such as great art, great stories, so that they would go on to do great things when they grew up. They did this by giving them inspiring lectures, showing them inspiring films and reading them inspiring stories.

The boys slept in dormitories, which were like old, cold classrooms with iron beds in them. Roald was not allowed to go to the toilet at night, so under his bed he had a kind of potty called a bedpan. There was no bathroom. He and the other boys washed in front of everyone else in the dormitory, using basins of cold water. Brrrr! If Roald woke up in the night, he could hear all the other boys breathing. Sometimes he could hear boys crying. Sometimes this was a place where he planned great tricks, like climbing out of the windows or hiding sweets and cakes. But sometimes this was a place where boys ganged up on other boys.

Nearly everybody Roald Dahl knew at school was male, apart from one or two teachers, his housemaster's wife and Matron, who was a sort of replacement mother while the boys were away from home. Some schoolboys really liked their matron. Others didn't. Not at all. Roald was one of those. In his first autobiography *Boy*, he says:

Looking back on it now, there seems little doubt that the Matron disliked small boys very much indeed. She never smiled at us or said anything nice, and when for example the lint stuck to the cut on your kneecap, you were not allowed to take it off yourself bit by bit so that it didn't hurt. She would always whip it off with a flourish, muttering, 'Don't be such a ridiculous little baby!'

When he first went to boarding school, Roald was very homesick. He slept in his bed the wrong way round, with his head near the window, so that he could look out across the Bristol Channel towards Llandaff, his home town in Wales, on the other side of the water. Once he was so homesick that he pretended to be seriously ill with appendicitis, which wasn't just an illness that would get him out of school for a couple of weeks, but an illness that meant a surgeon would slice him open and whip out his appendix. He wanted to go home *that* badly. In *Boy*, Roald says that the school sent him home, but the family doctor soon figured out that Roald was just pretending and so he and the doctor struck a deal: the doctor wouldn't say anything about Roald fibbing and would confirm that he had a real stomach infection – but only if Roald went back to the school.

I should say here that anyone writing about Roald Dahl's life has to be very, very careful about one thing. Roald sometimes told stories that were *not* completely and utterly true. As he once wrote, 'I don't lie. I merely make the truth a little more interesting . . . I don't break my word – I merely bend it slightly.'

So, did Roald *really* strike a deal with the doctor? Did he *really* fool Matron and his teachers that he had appendicitis? We'll never know for certain. My guess is that *something* like that happened, but as he told the story he added bits to it. And I think this because – *shhh* – I do the same thing when I write!

But what we *do* know is that Roald Dahl was

definitely homesick. In *Boy,* he says that for the whole of the first term he was homesick. He talks of the people looking after him – the headmaster, teachers and Matron – as if they were a mix of tyrants, dictators, swindlers and cranks.

Harald Dahl, 1863–1920

However you might be surprised about the sort of home he was homesick for, because his family was quite EXTRAORDINARY.

Although Roald had an English accent, his parents came from Norway. Before Roald was born, his father, Harald Dahl, decided to leave Norway and seek his fortune. He set up a new business in the thriving coal industry of South Wales. His mother, before she married Harald, was called Sofie Magdalene Hesselberg. Roald wasn't their first baby. Before him there were Astri and Alfhild. And, before that, Harald had had

Astri Dahl, 1912–20

two children with his first wife. They were called Ellen and Louis. Harald's first wife, whom he had loved very much, had died. So, Roald was number five and number six was Else. But then two terrible things happened. First, Astri died and then, soon after, Roald's father died too. Roald's mother was expecting a baby when her husband died. This was another daughter – Asta. And all this happened by the time Roald was still only three years old.

That's an awful lot of information to absorb in one go, but I think it's important to know about a person's background if you are to understand them. It's events like these that go to shape who a person is, and how he or she thinks. (If you'd like to see Roald Dahl's family tree, it's on page 20.)

Roald would have remembered very little of the tragedies, because he was so young when they happened. He must have grown up relying on his mother for stories about his father and his older sister. He would have heard stories *about* these people instead of having them as *real* people to know and to touch. And he would have had to imagine what they were like from the stories he had heard about them. This must have been a lot of work for his imagination. If we're looking for the different ingredients that made Roald Dahl into a storyteller, I think learning to imagine and learning to listen to stories are two of the most important.

And there's something else. These family stories weren't told to Roald in the language he used at school. They were told in Norwegian. Back then, he was bilingual – he could think and talk in two different languages – and there was hardly anyone he met in Britain who could speak his home language of Norwegian. He grew up knowing a sort of secret language, and it was in that secret language he would have learned about his father.

For those of us who speak just one language, how we speak and how we write are kind of invisible. We just do it. We don't have to think too much about which words to use, or why we use one word or another. And we don't have to think too much about how we say things. But people who are bilingual hop between their two languages and doing that hopping often stirs up questions about the words we use and why and how we use them.

Roald Dahl's mother

Roald's mother was a very important person in his life. She was right at the heart of the Dahl family. She was the one who kept things and people together. And she told stories. But she was also

the person who sent Roald away to school. So she was responsible for making him happy *and* making him feel homesick and sad.

Much later in his life, Roald often told interviewers that he thought children were quite able to love and hate their parents at the same time and that was why in his stories he wrote about parents or other grown-ups who are beastly, alongside others who are lovely. There are Matilda's parents and Miss Honey in *Matilda*. Or how about the witches and Grandmamma in *The Witches*? Roald Dahl was one of the first writers who created this mixture of good and bad parents in his children's books. You can find it in fairy tales like *Hansel and Gretel* and *Snow White and the Seven Dwarfs* but before Roald Dahl it was quite rare to find these beastly and lovely characters side by side in stories.

So that's what Roald Dahl's life was like when he was nine years old. I think it's quite unusual. You may recognize some bits of it. I hope you don't recognize others. But the good bits and the sad bits and the downright bizarre bits form the background of one of my favourite writers. And I think, together, they start to give an idea of why he went on to write such amazing books.

I'm going to end this chapter with a little story of my own.

When I think of Roald Dahl's childhood, I'm reminded of someone I knew very, very well: my own father. When my father was a little boy, about the same age as Roald, his parents split up and he never saw his dad again. So he also lost his dad. Like Roald, he was brought up in a household mostly full of women – his mother, his sister and his aunts. And, some of the time, there was a different language spoken at home. His mother told him they were different and that other people didn't believe the same things. This was sometimes a strange and uncomfortable feeling.

My dad said that all through his childhood, whenever he felt sad or angry or uncomfortable or different, he would dream that his father would suddenly turn up and make things better. He would stare at the photos of his father and listen to his mother's stories about him, about how good and clever he was. But it was always just the photos. No dad turned up. So my dad said that he had a secret inner life where he and his imaginary father lived.

My dad wasn't sent away to a boarding school, but his mother used to have to go into hospital for several weeks at a time, and, while she was away, he used to have nightmares in which she would die and he would have to live with the relatives he didn't like and who, he thought, didn't like him. And people around him told stories, some of them about ghosts and spirits called 'dybbuks' and a giant clay man called 'the Golem' who smashes up a whole city. Meanwhile, there was another place, another country, where his grandfather and some of his other relations came from, where it was said there were dangerous men on horses called 'Cossacks'...

And there the similarity ends, because my dad didn't grow up to be a famous writer like Roald Dahl. But he did become a storyteller and he did write about his own life. He also did a lot of other kinds of writing: he turned this inner life into thoughts about how best to teach and talk to children so that they would enjoy listening, reading and acting out stories. He kept thinking about the child he once was, imagining that quite a few of the children he was teaching were a bit like him, and wondering what kinds of stories and poems he and they might like. He wrote about languages other than English and he looked closely at how children speak and write.

So, when I think about Roald Dahl's childhood, I can't help but think how there were some things about both Roald and my father and their lives that were quite similar, and how perhaps that led them both to do things in life that were quite similar too.

I think that a childhood can sometimes last a lifetime.

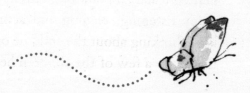

The Family Tree

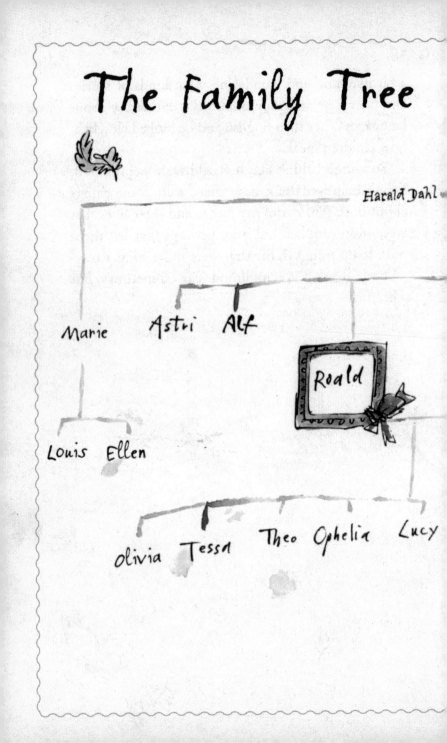

Harald Dahl

Marie   Astri   Alf

Roald

Louis Ellen

Olivia Tessa   Theo Ophelia Lucy

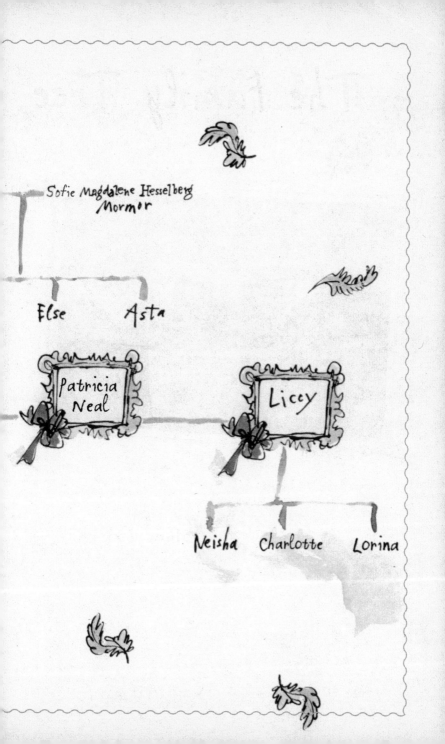

Llandaff Cathedral

Chapter 2
School Days

Harald Dahl, Roald's father, was a man who worked very hard for his living. He was a shipbroker. This didn't mean that he broke ships. It meant that he supplied boats to people who wanted to sell their goods to other countries and who needed to transport their goods there, by sea. Harald must have been a great success at his job, because by the time he died, when Roald was only three, he left a lot of money and property to his family. In today's money, they would have been worth a colossal £5 million.

Harald Dahl

This must have been a relief to Roald's mother, Sofie. Neither she nor any of her children would need to go without food or new clothes. Mrs Dahl could afford to employ servants – or help, as they were known – to do the washing, cleaning and cooking, and to look after the children. Roald and his sisters could probably have the toys they wanted, they had a big house and garden to live and play in, and went on lots of nice holidays too – sometimes in Wales or often in Norway with their relatives. And one thing his mother could certainly afford was to send Roald to expensive schools.

First, there was the kindergarten, or nursery, at Elmtree House in Llandaff, near Cardiff, where he went when he was six years old, in 1922. He was there for just one year. Then he went to Llandaff Cathedral School for two years. His next school was St Peter's, the boarding school in Weston-super-Mare, where he stayed until 1929, when he was thirteen. After that it was off to Repton, a famous public school not far from Derby in the Midlands, which he left in 1934, aged eighteen.

Thanks to Roald and his mother, we can travel back in time and find out more about his schooldays. This is because he kept his school reports and his mother kept the letters that he sent home to her. *Thank goodness*. That's a lot of valuable information about a boy who became a world-famous author.

One of the first glimpses we get of Roald's schooldays is at Elmtree House. Here, Roald was looked after and taught by two sisters, Mrs Corfield and Miss Tucker. He remembered his teachers as being 'sweet and smiling'.

Things were very different at his next school:

Llandaff Cathedral School. It stood next door to the — you've guessed it — cathedral. (In fact, it's still there, if you want to see where Roald went to school.) There was a proper headmaster in this place. And it was steeped in tradition — full of stories about itself, stretching back hundreds of years. Roald's two years at the school became full of stories for him too, especially the famous one he tells in *Boy* about the time he and his friends played a trick on a woman they thought was utterly, completely, totally horrible — Mrs Pratchett. She ran the local sweet shop and Roald's little gang from the cathedral school came to hate her . . .

She never smiled. She never welcomed us when we went in, and the only times she spoke were when she said things like, 'I'm watchin' you so keep yer thievin' fingers off them chocolates!' Or 'I don't want you in 'ere just to look around! Either you forks out or you gets out!'

But by far the most loathsome thing about Mrs Pratchett was the filth that clung around her. Her apron was grey and greasy. Her blouse had bits of breakfast all over it, toast-crumbs and tea stains and splotches of dried egg-yolk. It was her hands, however, that disturbed us most. They were disgusting. They were black with dirt and grime. They looked as though they had been putting lumps of coal on the fire all day long. And do not forget please that it was these very hands and fingers that she plunged into the sweet-jars when we asked for a pennyworth of Treacle Toffee or Wine Gums or Nut Clusters or whatever . . .

The other thing we hated Mrs Pratchett for was her meanness. Unless you spent a whole sixpence all in one go, she wouldn't give you a bag. Instead you got your sweets twisted up in a small piece of newspaper which she tore off a pile of old Daily Mirrors lying on the counter.

And *then* Roald says that he and his friends found a dead mouse under the floorboards, which gave him a wonderfully wicked idea.

'Why don't we,' I said, 'slip it into one of Mrs Pratchett's jars of sweets? Then when she puts her dirty hand in to grab a handful, she'll grab a stinky dead mouse instead.'

But how would they put the mouse into the sweet jar *without* Mrs Pratchett seeing? This called for a fiendishly clever plot. The 'Great Mouse Plot', in fact.

We were strutting a little as we entered the shop. We were the victors now and Mrs Pratchett was the victim. She stood behind the counter and her small malignant pig-eyes watched us suspiciously as we came forward.

'One Sherbet Sucker, please,' Thwaites said to her, holding out his penny.

I kept to the rear of the group, and when I saw Mrs Pratchett turn her head away for a couple of seconds to fish a Sherbet Sucker out of the box, I lifted the heavy glass lid of the Gobstopper jar and dropped the mouse in. Then I replaced the lid as silently as possible. My heart was thumping like mad and my hands had gone all sweaty.

'And one Bootlace, please,' I heard Thwaites saying.

When I turned round, I saw Mrs Pratchett holding out the Bootlace in her filthy fingers.

'I don't want all the lot of you troopin' in 'ere if only one of you is buyin',' she screamed at us. 'Now beat it! Go on, get out!'

As soon as we were outside, we broke into a run. 'Did you do it?' they shouted at me.

'Of course I did!' I said.

'Well done you!' they cried. 'What a super show!'

I felt like a hero. I was a hero. It was marvellous to be so popular.

Every time I read that story, I think about one thing: the word 'trick'. Here is Roald Dahl, less than nine years old, and what is he doing? Coming up with a trick! And that reminds me of the books he wrote. They are full of tricks, cunning plans and naughty jokes. If the story about the mouse and the sweet-shop lady is true (and we can never be absolutely, totally sure about that), and it really was Roald who came up with the 'Great Mouse Plot', then I think he had already begun to invent ways of writing.

Why?

Because if you plot and plan a trick, you need to think ahead and imagine 'What would happen if . . . ?' If you're someone who loves to imagine 'What would happen if . . . ?', such as 'What would happen if my best friend turned into cat . . . ?' then you're well on the way to being a writer. Roald wrote the story of what happened in the 'Great Mouse Plot' many, many years after it happened. But, in a way, he 'wrote' it when he and his friends looked at the dead mouse and imagined what they were going to do with it. He wasn't really writing it, of course, but he was thinking ahead, planning and imagining . . .

When I read the 'Great Mouse Plot', it made me wonder what kind of writer Roald Dahl was. When you write stories, you have to do all you can to grab your readers' attention. How does Roald do this here?

First of all, he tells us about Mrs Pratchett. But he doesn't just say 'Mrs Pratchett was horrible' and then move straight on to the plot. Instead, he shows us what's horrible about how she *looks*, the things she *says* and one key thing about her *character*, her meanness. In fact, he gives us such a thorough picture that we can start to imagine things about her that Roald Dahl does *not* tell us, like what she might think of this group of boys coming into her shop. Does she think *they* are horrible? But why would she think that? What might they have done? What *else* is Dahl not telling us?

I also noticed that Roald does what can be called 'inside-outside'. This is where a writer tells some of the story as if he were a fly on the wall, watching everyone from the outside, but at other times he goes 'inside' a character to tell the story from their point of view. This keeps our minds busy, flipping to and fro between outside and inside. One moment we're *looking* at what's going on and the next we're *listening*. Just like this. We *hear* Roald say to his friends, 'Then when she puts her dirty hand in to grab a handful, she'll grab a stinky dead mouse instead . . .' And he *describes* the scene: 'We were strutting a little as we entered the shop.' This mix of listening and looking also makes us want to follow the story and to enjoy getting the whole picture.

At first glance, the 'Great Mouse Plot' might look one-dimensional. This means that the story is not complicated: in this case, that it's just about goodies and baddies – Mrs Pratchett is a baddy and the boys are getting their own back on her. 'Serves her right!' we might say. And that's all there is to it. But, if you are a really good storyteller, you can turn a one-dimensional story into something that readers will wonder about. I think that good writing will always give you a chance to look at things from different points of view, rather as if you were seeing a scene first from the front and then from behind, or first from inside one person's head and then from inside another person's.

One thing that none of them – not Roald, nor his friends – seems to have thought about was what would happen to them if their terrible mouse crime were found out. And this was . . . PUNISHMENT.

I'm sure you know about punishment. You probably know of people – even you! – who have been sent out of the classroom . . . or made to stay in at breaktime . . . or been given a detention . . . or sent to see the head teacher . . . or even been excluded from school altogether. What's absolutely NOT allowed is for anyone in school to hit you. But when I was at school and, before that, when Roald was at school, teachers were allowed to punish children by hitting them. They could use all sorts of things – their bare hands, sticks, belts, rulers, blackboard rubbers, shoes – and they could hit a child in all sorts of places – round the face, across the hand or on their backside. Sometimes they did it when they were angry, while we were sitting at our desks. Sometimes we were called out to the front of the class and they did it in front of everyone. Sometimes they just threw things at us. When I was at secondary school I had one teacher who used to yank my hair, pulling my head down to the desk. Then he'd let go. But, before I could lift my head up, the teacher would turn his hand into a fist and then punch the back of my head. Another one – a very nice man, actually – walloped me round the face.

Caning was one thing that bothered Roald Dahl more than any other about school. It leaps out of the pages of his books. He wanted all of his readers to know he HATED being caned. He says that plenty of his teachers were 'cane-happy', but there was one particular way of dishing out this punishment that always felt very serious and solemn. This was when you were called to the headmaster's office. Just imagine standing nervously on his carpet, perhaps daring to look around his office at the old photos and books, the chairs and the desk while you waited. Aside from your own parents, the headmaster was probably the most important person you knew, and this special, clever and important person had chosen you for this extra-special thing: to beat you because you had misbehaved. And there was always something you had to do before you were beaten: you had to make some part of yourself available so that he could hit it. Every boy knew by heart the words 'Hold out your hand' or 'Bend over'. These were words that were said over and over again, and they set in motion a series of moves that always happened in the same way, with the same quiet, solemn tone to it all.

The teachers told themselves that they were trying to make you a better person. It happened to me at primary school because I and some other boys ran after a ball into the girls' playground, then booed a teacher who tried to take the ball. And, Roald tells us, this kind of punishment happened to him and his friends at school. In fact, he spent a good deal of one book, *Matilda*, showing us one teacher in particular, Miss Trunchbull, who loved beating children. He made her so horrible and so cruel that many people – and, I've noticed, especially children – laugh. One part that people laugh at a lot is when she throws a boy out of the window.

This doesn't mean that Roald thought the beating stuff didn't matter. Just the opposite, in fact. He thought it mattered a great deal. He hated it so much that one of the ways he could deal with his feelings was to turn it into a story and exaggerate it, making it so big that readers end up thinking it's funny. Writers for children had made punishment funny before – in the Billy Bunter books and in comics like *The Beano*. What's really unusual and special about Roald is that he was one of the first writers for children to get us all thinking that this sort of punishment was both funny and wrong *at the same time*.

But the point about the beating is that it was supposed to hurt. It hurt Roald and it hurt his friends in the 'Great Mouse Plot'. They secretly showed each other their wounds. In a school where children were regularly beaten, it wasn't spoken about in public, but *everyone* spoke about it in private. Some children made secret plans on how to make it hurt less (like stuffing a book down your trousers). Then there were stories about what you could put on your skin before and after (vinegar, turps, olive oil). There were also mind-games people talked about, ways of making yourself think it didn't hurt so much or ways of showing the teacher you didn't care. There were even stories of children who hit the teacher back! And there was the big, big deal about what to tell your parents, what they would say when you told them and what they actually did . . .

This is what Roald's mother did. She saw the marks that the cane had made on Roald's skin – the scarlet stripes, as he called them – and she took him away from Llandaff Cathedral School at once.

Roald Dahl's Schools

Elmtree House, 1922–23
Kindergarten
Age 6–7
Llandaff, Cardiff, Wales

NOW CLOSED

Llandaff Cathedral School, 1923–5
Preparatory school
Age 7–9
Llandaff, Cardiff, Wales

STILL OPEN

St Peter's School, 1925–9
Preparatory school
Age 9–13
Weston-super-Mare,
Somerset, England

CLOSED

Then and Now

Repton, 1929–34
Independent school
Age 13–17
Repton, Derbyshire, England

THE PRIORY HOUSE,
REPTON,
DERBY.

Dear Mama
Thanks awfully
and your letters. We
last night. We fried
hieny beans over the
cream. Those bis
Last night we
there is about

March 23rd. 1930.

Dear Mama,

Thanks awfully for your letter, and the parcel, an
one egg had a crack around it, exactly the same as one
some of the slime had come out, and I had two of them
were excellent, in the form of poached eggs on toast
At the beginning of the week we had another leavy
now the weather is beginning starting to look more
There have been a lot of sports last week, notably the
high jumping; the two from each of the ten houses ha
string. I had to jump for Priory, and I don't know
with Henderson, and Bell we also won the senior
very shaky, though, jumping in front of most of the
had when it was over.

Your

Dear Mama
        I am having a lovely time here.   23ᵗⁿ Spt
& We play foot ball every day here. The beds
the beds have no springs. Will you send my
stamp   album, and quite a lot of swops.
The   masters are very nice. I've
got all my clothes in a now, & and a belt,
and, ties, and a school school Jersy.
        love from
            Boy

Chapter 3

Letters

The next thing that happened to Roald was that the amazing Mrs Dahl, who'd just rescued him from the local school, packed him off to boarding school instead. As you know from the first chapter, St Peter's was on the other side of the Bristol Channel – a big stretch of water where the River Severn becomes the sea. Roald travelled with his mother to school on a paddle steamer that chugged across the water, going the rest of the way by taxi. And then she left him there.

Roald was nine years old and he was on his own. Here's the very first letter that he wrote home from St Peter's in 1925. It makes me wonder what I would have written to my mother in his situation. What do you think of it? I've left in the spelling mistakes because they're funny!

Dear Mama   23rd Sept

I am having a lovely time here. We play football every day here. The beds have no springs. Will you send my stamp album, and quite a lot of swops. The masters are very nice. I've got all my clothes now, and a belt, and, tie, and a school Jersey.

Love from
Boy

At first glance it might look a bit dull – and maybe not a letter from the future Fantastic Mr Dahl. Where are the jokes? Where's the story about a horrible, crazy teacher or some awful boy at the school? It doesn't tell us very much about the young Roald . . . or does it? Let's look at the letter again, this time as if we're detectives searching for clues. Because it's a valuable piece of evidence.

First, he calls his mother **Mama**, which reminds us that Roald had strong ties to another country: Norway. Then he says that he's having a **lovely time**. Hmm, I wonder! Later, he did have some really good times at St Peter's, but I can't help thinking that the very first moments wouldn't have been *lovely*. And, in *Boy*, he tells us very clearly and strongly that his first moments were anything but.

'I had never spent a single night away from our large family before,' he says. *'I was left standing there beside my brand new trunk and my brand new tuck-box. I began to cry.'*

So why does he tell Mama that he's having a lovely time? Maybe his teacher had told him what to write but I like to think he's making sure at first that she doesn't worry about him. Don't you?

Then he tells Mama that they play **football** every day. This didn't mean that he and the other boys were just kicking a ball about in the playground. Instead, it would have been an organized game on the school field. Roald grew to really like sport and as a newcomer he must have already spotted that it was a big deal at St Peter's.

He goes on to tell Mama that the **beds have no springs**. When I was nine, the springs were broken on my bed and I was always complaining to my parents about it and moaning that my brother's bed was more comfortable than mine! Maybe, in a way, I was getting all moany and whingy about the fact that having a lumpy bed proved that my parents didn't care enough about me to get me a nice comfy bed! Is young Roald trying to send Mama a message that he doesn't think she's done enough to make sure he's comfy at night?

Then it's on to **stamps**. All his life, Roald was a great collector. If you go to the Roald Dahl Museum and Story Centre in Great Missenden you can see some of the things he collected, including a ball he made out of the silver wrapping gathered from the many chocolate bars he ate! Squirrels collect nuts. They bury them in the ground so that when winter comes and there's no food they can go round digging them up. I think writers are a bit like that. We collect stuff so that when we're searching for inspiration we can look at our collections and – hey presto! – ideas might pop into our heads. It would have been very easy for Roald to collect stamps – he had foreign relatives who would have sent letters and parcels covered in exciting stamps, with pictures of intriguing foreign places, kings, queens and famous people. This might have impressed all the boys Roald was meeting. What's more, he had 'swops'. These were double copies (or more) of any stamp, which could be swapped with other boys' stamps in order to make his collection even better. A great future in both collecting and looking good among his friends was opening up straight away, so long as Mama sent them.

Next Roald tells his mother that the **masters are very nice**. I doubt it. In 1925 the masters of private boarding schools were all sorts of things, but on the whole I've never heard them called 'nice'. Is Roald trying to reassure Mama it's not like the other school where he got beaten really badly? When young children see anxious looks on their parents' faces, some think that it's their job to get rid of that worry, even if it means making up a little story to do so. Perhaps Roald was trying to convince her that everything was all right, *even when it wasn't*. Anyone who learns how to do that is well on their way to becoming a storyteller!

Finally, Roald finishes the letter with his nickname, 'Boy'. In his new world, where everyone called him 'Roald', it must have been a relief to use a name that no one else at school knew about. 'Boy' was his home name and must have reminded him and his mother of how much they loved each other.

Love from
~~Boy~~ Boy

In *Boy* Roald says their letters were censored. This meant each boy had to show his letter to a teacher so that he could point out any spelling mistakes. But, secretly, Roald thought that the teachers were checking up on them, making sure that the boys didn't complain to their parents about the food or being badly treated.

Here's Roald's second letter, which was written only two days later:

Dear Mama

Thank you for the stamps. I've swoped quite a lot. I played football yesterday, and scored one goal. We went for a walk today but it was not a very long one. I am going to write to Bestemama and Bestepapa and tante Ellen. I doant think I want eny moor stamps. I've got my straw hat. I had it yesterday. I hope Mike will get better soon. Thank Else, and Alfhild, and baby for thire letters. I can understand your writing very well. I am very glad you found my boat.

I like this letter a lot. I like the way Roald includes his Norwegian relatives – Bestemama and Bestepapa are his mother's parents, Roald's grandparents. I like the way he remembers that Mike's ill (I think Mike could be a pet but I'm not entirely sure); the way he reassures Mama that he can decipher her handwriting, so can understand her letters; the way that he is telling her how glad he is that she's looking after his things back home; and I also like his occasionally dodgy spelling.

I enjoy the fact that the letter hints that Mama has sent him a whacking great pile of stamps – too many by the sound of it – so he doesn't need 'eny moor'. And now he's got what might have struck Mama as being one of the most English things ever: a straw hat. It would have been a boater – a hard, flat straw hat with a ribbon around it.

It occurs to me that this letter is strong on empathy – that's the ability to understand and feel what other people feel. All writers need empathy. They need to be able to imagine what other people think and feel so that they can write about them, and they need to be able to guess what readers would like to know. In Roald's letter, I can hear loudly and clearly that he's trying to figure out what Mama would like to hear, and he's trying to think about his relatives and Mike. Funnily enough, some people have said that Roald Dahl the writer was sometimes short of empathy, that he made too many people in his books into people we just hate or despise. Think of George's grandmother in *George's Marvellous Medicine*, Miss Trunchbull and Matilda's parents in *Matilda*, the landowner in *Danny the Champion of the World*, the witches in *The Witches*, Boggis in *Fantastic Mr Fox* and even the crocodile in *The Enormous Crocodile*. But saying that these characters are just hateful or that they prove Roald the writer didn't show empathy misses the point, I think. As he was writing, Roald Dahl was always asking himself what kinds of things children would like reading about. (He also thought a good deal about why they might enjoy them too.) He was showing empathy for children by inventing characters and scenes that they would enjoy. Anyway, apart from that, he was also someone who did more than show us horrible people being defeated; he also tried to show people's kindness and love or their kind and loving deeds – there's Miss Honey in *Matilda*, Grandmamma in *The Witches*, Danny and his father in *Danny the Champion of the World* and even Mr Fox in *Fantastic Mr Fox*. That needs empathy too.

In the four years Roald was at St Peter's he had a big advantage when it came to sport and that was his height. Because he was taller than the other boys – one school report called him 'overgrown' – he was a useful player in the rugby team. He did well at boxing and also enjoyed cricket and football. In his letters, he talks a lot about his sporting achievements, telling Mama things like:

> '*I hit two sixes . . . One hit the pavilion with a tremendous crash and just missed a window.*'

Oops.

But sometimes his studies didn't go very well. 'He imagines he is doing badly and consequently does badly,' said one teacher's report. At that school, if you did badly, it meant that you were kept in the same class for another year, with younger pupils. The danger of being kept back a year must have bothered Roald quite a lot, because some of his letters are just lists of where he is in each class for the different subjects, like the one opposite, written in November 1926.

There are several letters like this. I get the feeling that Roald, his mother and the school cared a great deal about learning, study, tests and marks.

> ## Dear Mama
>
> This is my order,
> French = 6th
> Latin = 3rd
> grammar and composition = 5th
> General Knolidge = 1st
> Geometry = 1st
> Divinity = 2nd
> History = 5th
> Arithmetic = 1st
> Algebra = 1st
> Geography = 3rd
> There are 14 boys in the form.
> I am first in the three maths.
>
> Love from
> Roald

One of his old school friends, Douglas, noticed that there was something quite different about Roald and said, 'He was very much an immigrant from Norway. I was an immigrant from Turkey . . . we were both foreigners.' This seems to have brought them together. The two boys used to walk together on school trips into the local town of Weston-super-Mare, talking about the school's 'stupid or unnecessary rules', as they put it. But they didn't just whinge. They liked playing with the English language too, making up word games. And this reminds me of *The BFG*. Every time I read it, I think that *The BFG* is a book written by someone who liked having fun with words, with how they sound and how you can make up new ones.

Douglas also says that his friend was brilliant at conkers and in one letter Roald told his mother that he was the school champion because he had 'the highest conker in the school – 273'. This meant that Roald's conker had won a phizz-whizzing 273 times!

In his letters, Roald also talked about collecting things from the great outdoors, like birds' eggs (this is absolutely forbidden now – do not do it unless you actually want to be arrested). Altogether, he collected 172, all carefully laid out in a special glass cabinet with ten drawers, ranging from the eggs of a little tiny bird like the wren up to the eggs of big birds like gulls and crows.

But, besides collecting and conkers, there was something else that Roald was becoming good at: writing.

His letters start to fill up with loving descriptions of the things he sees and finds. And he spends pages telling his mother the latest fabulous things he has just learned in school – especially anything to do with animals and birds. He and the other boys were shown films that fired his imagination. In one, a pilot flew to the Cape of Good Hope in South Africa (it may not seem like a world-shattering event now, but this was in the very early days of flying) and in another he learned about climbing Mount Everest. They watched a film about a long-distance car journey to India and Tibet, and another showing ants fighting a centipede and flipping a woodlouse on its back.

Roald Dahl was a writer of extremes – he liked writing about amazing, odd, extraordinary and exaggerated things. When reading some of his letters, I can't help feeling that he was always on the lookout for bizarre events. There was the trip to the caves in Cheddar Gorge near his school, when Roald and the others were crammed into an open-top coach called a charabanc. Once in Weston-super-Mare there was a gas explosion, which started a terrible fire that burned down three shops – Roald went the next day to inspect the damage. Perhaps Mama liked to hear about them. Perhaps he liked to write about them. But, if something worth writing about happened, then that's what he did.

It's not surprising that if there was anything to do with storytelling at school, Roald loved it. In November 1925 he wrote to his mother about a lecture on 'bird legends' and he tells her the Aesop fable of how the wren became king of the birds, and another of how the blackbird got black feathers and a yellow beak.

One of Roald's favourite speakers was Major Cottam, who seems to have been quite a showman. The Major features quite often in Roald's letters, reading and reciting, and that conjures up for me an interesting picture: a man with a military background – I wonder, did he wear his uniform? – acting out stories and poems to groups of the boys, fascinating them, making them laugh, fall silent and be thoroughly amazed as he brought great books to life.

Last night about seven o'clock Major Cottam recited 'The Merchant of Venice' on the field under the trees, he was awfuly funny, and then he recited a little Sweedish poem and then a famous poem from Kiplin, 'Gounga-Dedn', it was awfuly funny, he acts as well while he is reciting.

Just before Christmas in 1926, when he's ten, Roald writes:

On friday we had a topping lecture in Esqimaux, all the slides were coloured, it was very interesting. And today we are having a cinamatograph on Dr Banardos Homes . . .

We had a special treat last night, we all hung up our stockings, and when it was dark matron came in dressed up as father Xmas, and put things in our stockings, I got a kind of musical box and a soldier on a horse in mine. The same night she hung up hers outside her door and we all put things in it, it was full in the end. We start Exams next Tuesday and they go on till Thursday. I AM COMING HOME NEXT FRIDAY ON THE 17TH OF DECEMBER, BY the 1.36 (one thirty six) train, please meet me.

So, if Matron dressed up as Father Christmas, maybe she wasn't quite as bad as he made out in *Boy* . . . ? And I like the capital letters too. Is he reminding Mama to be there? Is it possible that she sometimes forgot to meet him?

Another topic that really seemed to interest Roald was anything to do with illness and accidents, and all the different medicines and cures too. Here's a letter he wrote on 6 October 1929:

My headaches have quite gone now. I had one all the first week of the term, and I thought I would try 'Mistol'. So I did, I fairley poured it down for two days and it developed into a bad cold which I soon got rid of with that worthy muck. And now if I ever get the slightest head, I take a go of Mistol and it goes. What do you think it was? Hayfever perhaps. There are now a lot of colds about, and several boys in the sick room, so I think there will be flu soon, (there might not be of course), but after all that I have nearly finished my bottle of mistol, so please send me another, because I don't want flu this term, for the Common Entrance is on the 12th November.

It sounds as if young Roald has already learned – or thinks that he's learned – to take control. Today, children don't dose themselves up with medicine because that would be very dangerous. But back then Roald was pouring it down his throat. He figures that the medicine is making him better and keeping the flu away. It wasn't doing anything of the sort. That's just his imagination. But a belief in special, magic potions is very handy if you want to write books. And I can't stop myself thinking about a certain George and some *marvellous medicine* . . . can you?

Roald Dahl was also developing an eye for detail. During a royal visit to Weston-super-Mare, what interested him most was the fact that a train ran over someone and a local shopkeeper became so excited that he fired six shots into the air and terrified the royals!

When he writes to his sister Alfhild, he says:

The barber is a very funny man, his name is Mr Lundy, when I went to have my hair cut last Monday, a lot of spiders came out from under the cupboard and he stepped on them and there was a nasty squashy mess on the floor.

> In the Drill Display we have a Pyramid, there are a lot a boys standing in the shape of a star fish and some boys in the middle and a boy standing on one of the boys shoulders with his hands out, it looks very nice.

No one becomes a writer overnight. Just as actors rehearse their parts over and over again before we see them in plays and films, and sports people practise their movements, strokes, aims and tackles, so writers practise their writing – perhaps without even realizing it. It doesn't seem as if ten-year-old Roald knew that he was going to be a writer, but nevertheless he was practising and not just in lessons.

His letters home were giving him the chance to see what sounded good and what worked. He was finding out what sorts of things grabbed his mother's and his sisters' attention. And he was learning what made them laugh. Many years later, Roald discovered that his mother had secretly kept every single one of his letters to her. Isn't that amazing? I think this shows how proud she was of her young son, and how much she missed him.

And there's something else a young writer needs to do: read lots of different books. Before he went to St Peter's, Roald had read Beatrix Potter's stories.

He liked *Winnie-the-Pooh* by A. A. Milne, *The Secret Garden* by Frances Hodgson Burnett and the fairytales of Hans Christian Andersen, such as *The Snow Queen*. He also liked Hilaire Belloc's *Cautionary Verses*, which he learned off by heart. If you compare Roald Dahl's *Dirty Beasts* and *Revolting Rhymes* with *Cautionary Verses*, you can see that in some ways he wrote in Hilaire Belloc's style.

At St Peter's, he began to read Shakespeare's plays, novels by Charles Dickens and Robert Louis Stevenson's *Treasure Island*. And he loved rollicking adventure stories by authors with wonderful names like H. Rider Haggard. Roald and his friend Douglas moved on to ghost stories and they were soon reading and talking about the scary stories of Edgar Allan Poe. It's clear that he and his fellow pupils were expected to read a lot and read very widely.

Many times he wrote home to tell his mother about the exams he had to do. On one occasion, he challenged her to answer one of the exam questions.

He says that he got most of these right:

In what books do the following carecters occur and give the authors:—

Beccey Sharp
Sam Weller
Beetle

Mowgli
Israel Hands
Athos
Jean Val Sican

Complete the following proverbs:-

A little learning . . .
A Rolling stone . . .
Bird in the Hand . . .
A sticth in time . . .

One job that a writer has to do is to help their readers see and feel what things are like. And one way of doing this is by using metaphors and similes. When talking about the charabanc that took them to the caves in Cheddar Gorge, Roald wrote that they were packed in *'like sardins in a tin'*, which is a simile. And here are the closing words that Roald wrote in his very last letter home from St Peter's:

Please excuse this bad writing, but I am writing it in Prep, under rather bad conditions, also, an excuse is that someone is singing downstairs, and the noise closely resembles that of a flys' Kneecap, rattled about in a bilious buttercup, both having Kidny trouble and lumbago.

These sound to me like the words of a boy who loves language. This is a boy who is trying hard – maybe a little too hard – to think up similes that sound weird, funny and amazing. And this is a boy who is thoroughly enjoying doing it.

Roald Dahl's Letters

Jan 19th 1926

Dear Mama

I got to school all right. Please send my music book as quick as posible. Don't forget to tell Smiths to send "Bubbles".

Love from
Boy

POST CARD

Mrs Dahl

Cumberland Lodge
Llandaff
Nr Cardiff.

St Peter's
Weston-super-mare.

Jan. 27th 1928.

Dear Mama

Thank you very much for the cake etc. I got the book the day before yesterday, quite a nice edition. How are the chicks? hope they'll all live. By the way, you said she would'nt get any.

Here are a few more of Roald Dahl's letters to his
mother from St Peter's.

St. Peter's
Weston-super-mare.
March 24th 1926.

Dear Else

I will soon be coming home,
I am coming by train next Wednesday.
There is a craze for darts and
gliders, nearly every one has got
one, I have got one topping one,
it glides like anything. a boy
called Huntly-Wood made it for
me. I have got five quarter-

stars, I got one of them to day,
it was for writing from Mr Francis.
I think the French Play was very
good, and very funny as well, I
could not understand much of it.
but I think every one liked it.

Love from

BOY

Oct. 15th 1929.
St. Peter's.
Weston-super-mare.

Dear Mama

Thanks awfully for the Roller skates,
they are topphole. Were they the largest pair? at full
stretch they fit topppingly, but if my feet grow
much more they wont fit. We skate on the yard; we
had a toy fine time last night after tea; You see, the
chaps who haven't got pairs, pull you. At one time
I had eight chaps pulling me with a long rope, at
a terrific tick, and, I sat down in the middle of
it; my bottom is all p blue now! We also have "trains";
You get about ten chaps to pull, and with a long rope,
and all the roller-skaters hang on to each other,
and go around; but if one chap falls, all the ones
behind him come on top of him; the yard is

getting quite smooth now.

Last Wednesday we played a school called "Clarence" and
beat them on 5-1. So far we have played 3 matches
and won them all; hope we have as good a term as
the Prosser.

Last Sunday we had a lantern lecture on Lighthouses; the
man, gave pictures of the "Wolf", "Eddystone" the Bishops Rock,
and longships at Landsend, All of which we saw last
hols.

By the way, I had a birthday present from Mervali
yesterday. I was a thing called a "Yoo Yoh", which
runs up and down on a string, but is very hard to work.
It is very fascinating, but she confessed that it was
bought at Woolworths; and she said that it was the
craze there. I show you when, I get home.
Can you send me another tube of Gibbs tooth paste please.
Love from Roald

The beach at Nevlunghavn

Chapter 4

Holidays

Roald Dahl aged eight

Roald didn't just come across stories at school. For him, the holidays were crammed with strange and wonderful events too. By the time he was eleven, his mother and sisters had moved from Wales to a house in Bexley in Kent, about fifteen miles from London. It sounds a beautiful place, with a tennis court and grounds so huge that his mother had a gardener to look after them. In the house, there was even a special room for playing billiards.

In the 1920s many people as rich as the Dahls were very keen on behaving 'properly'. They had perfect manners, they wore the right clothes for every occasion, they spoke very politely and never ever said rude words or made rude noises. A lot of attention was paid to being clean – clean rooms, clean clothes, clean hair, clean face, clean hands – and any kind of shouting or running was strictly reserved for sport. Every day followed a special schedule, with breakfast, lunch and tea happening exactly on time. Boys were supposed to behave in one kind of a way and girls in another. There were also things that were 'proper' to read and see (and a lot of things that weren't). It was as if there were invisible rules. And people who didn't stick to the rules were frowned upon.

Did the Dahl family behave like this at home? Not at all. It seems as if Roald's mother didn't mind the children running about all over the place. She didn't appear to be bothered about them saying rude words, climbing trees or doing naughty and dangerous things. They were unconventional – they weren't like other people and they didn't stick to the rules. One story that the Dahl family liked to tell was how young Roald got himself an airgun, persuaded his sister to climb up a tree and then shot at her! In January 1928 he wrote to his mother, 'Please can you send my blank cartridge revolver, everybody here has one, including Highton and no one minds.' Years later, Roald told the story of how he once rigged up a kind of chariot on a wire so that he could water-bomb passers-by with water from old soup tins.

There weren't many mums like Mrs Dahl. It rather looks as if she thought that being naughty and wild was absolutely fine and part of how a child learns.

Maybe this is one of the reasons that Roald and Mama got on so well. In one of his letters, Roald even tells her this: 'We've got a new Matron called Miss Farmer in place of Miss Turner who left last term, one night in the washing room, having inspected a boy called Ford, she KISSED HIM.'

One thing we know about Roald Dahl, both from his books and from real life, was that he was quite naughty and wild himself. Most of us are held back by invisible rules, but Roald wasn't. Something gave him the confidence to say, write and do things that plenty of other people thought were shocking – think what the BFG did when he visited the Queen! I believe that it was Mrs Dahl who helped to give him this confidence.

'Stinky snozzcumbers,' the BFG said.

The school holidays weren't just spent at home. At Easter, the Dahls would pack their bags and go away. One place they went to was Tenby in South Wales. This is a beautiful Victorian seaside town, with an old harbour and long sandy beaches. Here, Roald could collect his eggs and starfish and go donkey riding. There was an island just off the coast with an ancient monastery on it and Roald would take a boat out to explore. Mrs Dahl used to rent a house overlooking the harbour for the family to stay in.

But for the Dahls there was an even more magical place: Norway. In *Boy*, Roald lovingly tells the story of how a great group of them travelled for several days to get there.

We were always an enormous party. There were my three sisters and my ancient half-sister (that's four), and my half-brother and me (that's six), and my mother (that's seven), and Nanny (that's eight) and in addition to these, there were never less than two others who were some sort of anonymous ancient friends of the ancient half-sister (that's ten altogether).

And, as Roald reminds us, they all spoke Norwegian.

Bestepapa Hesselberg

In a way, he says, 'going to Norway every summer was like going home'.

After a long, long journey, this large family group, with all their trunks and bags, would first visit the house in Oslo where Mrs Dahl's father and mother – Bestepapa and Bestemama – and her two sisters lived. Here, they ate old-style Norwegian food, with piles of fresh fish and home-made ice cream with little chips of crisp burnt toffee mixed into it, while the grown-ups drank and toasted each other over and over again, calling out, '*Skaal!*'

Next, they were off to the seaside! The Norwegian coastline is a magical place full of islands and fjords – long, narrow inlets where the mountainsides are steep and the water is very, very deep. In summer, the water is stunningly blue and the mountain slopes are covered in dark green pine forests. If ever you get the chance to visit the coast of Norway, you will see how beautiful and mysterious it is.

The fjords were full of fish and Roald loved to spend hours and hours in a boat, often with Louis, his half-brother, fishing and sunbathing. When he was older,

Mrs Dahl got hold of an old motorboat. It was 'a small and not very seaworthy white wooden vessel which sat far too low in the water and was powered by an unreliable one-cylinder engine'. It doesn't sound very safe, does it? But Roald and the

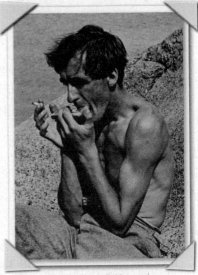
Louis Dahl

others headed up the fjord, hunting for different islands where they could go rock-pooling, fishing, swimming, diving and exploring, looking at the 'wooden skeletons of shipwrecked boats', feeding off wild strawberries and mussels and watching the 'shaggy, long-haired goats'. Sometimes, the sea was rough and it became pretty dangerous for the little party in this not-very-good boat. But Roald lived to tell the tale.

At night, Roald's mother told stories – sometimes made up, sometimes myths, legends and fairy tales, sometimes the stories of famous Norwegian writers who wrote about the kind of lonely, difficult lives people and animals had in this landscape of forests, mountains, rivers and fjords. She told of Norse gods who fought with giants in battles that lasted for days and weeks on end. There were tales of boys who outwitted wicked trolls, and of giant insects and giant frogs and cloud monsters, and of the hare who laughed till his jaws cracked and the tabby cat who ate too much. It was fantastic, magical, amazing, weird, scary, exciting stuff.

All this must have helped Roald Dahl to feel wonderfully different, in a good way. He was experiencing both a very proper English education *and* traditional Norwegian life. He doesn't seem to have known anyone outside his family who shared this particular mix of cultures. Being different can

Fishing on the Oslofjord

be very important for a writer. It can make you want to write about what it feels like to be you. It can make you want to write about the things that everyone else takes for granted, but which you see in a different way. Sometimes, it just makes you want to tell people about strange, different places and ways of life. Next time you think of the Big Friendly Giant, you might want to read some of the wonderful Norse myths or look at pictures of the coast of Norway and think about a young boy in his boat, far out on the fjord, looking down into the clear water, thinking, wondering, dreaming, planning and collecting.

Time is something that every writer needs. Time to think, wonder, dream, plan and collect. And Roald Dahl had plenty of that.

Roald, Alfhild, Else – Norway, 1924

Roald Dahl and Food

As well as chocolate, Roald Dahl loved to eat (and drink) many other things too. Here are just a few of them.

Roald Dahl's favourite foods of all time

Norwegian prawns
Lobster
Caviar
Scrumptious roast beef

Roald Dahl's favourite pudding

'*Krokaan* is simply a kind of crispy, crunchy toffee made from butter, sugar and almonds, and quite apart from the fact that its taste is so beguiling, it makes a most satisfying crunchy noise when you chew it. Ice cream, whatever flavour it is, is invariably a soft and silent meal, but when you fill it with krokaan chips, it suddenly becomes something that goes crunch when you chew instead of just floating silently down your throat.'

Roald Dahl's favourite soup

'*Chłodnik* is a cold Polish soup with a beetroot base and a number of other special ingredients, including chunks of lobster. It is the greatest soup that I have ever tasted, ice-cold, creamy and with a flavour so subtle and enticing that you feel you want to go on eating it forever.'

Roald Dahl's favourite family breakfast

Hot-house Eggs
Cut a circle out of a slice of bread. Pop the bread into a frying pan and cook on both sides in a little butter. Crack the egg into the hole in the bread – the white will spill over the edges very slightly to glue the egg in place. Flip the whole thing over and cook briefly on the other side.
'We always called it Hot-house Eggs,' said Roald Dahl. 'Don't ask me why.'

Roald Dahl's favourite workday lunch

Gin and tonic
Norwegian prawns with mayonnaise and lettuce
Kit Kat

A favourite supper of Roald Dahl's

Plump grilled Dover sole straight out of the Atlantic
Faintly green Portuguese wine
Almond tart

School dinners at Repton

Chapter 5

Teenage Years

In 1930 the teenage Roald Dahl was a new boy all over again, at Repton – the big, old public school for boys near Derby. There was a uniform, of course. But now it sounds more like fancy dress – striped trousers, a waistcoat, a long jacket called a tailcoat, a shirt with a stiff collar that had to be fixed to the shirt with special metal studs, very shiny black shoes and, finally, a boater. It must have taken a *long* time to get dressed.

Roald's house was called The Priory and about fifty boys lived there, with twelve from each year. Unlike at St Peter's, it really *was* a house, separate from the school in the town of Repton. The housemaster, Mr Jenkyns – the boys called him 'Binks' – and his family lived there too. Roald liked him a lot.

For the younger boys at this school and many like it, the real terror was in the way their lives were run by the older boys. At Repton, they ran a system where the oldest boys used the younger boys as their servants or,

73

Mr and Mrs Jenkyns and the boys from Priory House.
Roald Dahl is on the right of the second row from the front.

as Dahl called them, 'personal slaves'. Their way of keeping the younger boys in line was to beat them over and over again. So a new schoolboy started off being a slave who was caned and ended up being a slave-master, beating the next new lot of youngsters coming in. It was a sort of training in bullying. But the schoolmasters of the time thought that it was a training in leadership instead. What do *you* think?

In *Boy*, Roald tells us how much he hated all the bullying and beatings and nastiness. And, if you think the book sounds bad, you'll be stunned to know that when he first wrote *Boy* the descriptions sounded even worse. There, in full gory detail, he told the story of how the older boys once dumped him – fully dressed – into a cold bath and held his head under the water. But here's the strangest thing. In one draft Roald says that, after the beatings, the boys didn't sympathize with each other. Instead, they 'developed a curiously detached attitude to these vile tortures in order to preserve their sanity'. He says, if they had gathered around each other helping each other, 'I think we would all have broken down.'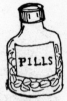

As we have seen, illness is something that Roald worried about a lot. Whether he was really ill or not isn't totally clear. In his letters home, he was always asking his mother to send him pills, lozenges, ointments and medicines of all kinds. He complains of corns, coughs, colds, headaches, constipation, weak bones . . . and there was even some conversation about him having a weak heart. At school, it was Matron who dealt with any serious illnesses, but when it came to things like cough medicine, the boys looked after themselves. Roald definitely did that. And, because of all his letters home, the view in the Dahl family was that he was not a very well chap.

Roald's teachers had a *lot* to say about him and not all of it good. Unlike his teachers at St Peter's, one thought that he was 'curiously dense and slow', another that he went in for 'fits of childishness' and 'fits of the sulks'. One found him a 'persistent muddler, writing and saying the opposite of what he means'. Other teachers said that he was idle, stupid, obstinate and too pleased with himself. Perhaps he was some of those things or perhaps he was just turning into a teenage rebel. We will never know.

But what we *do* know about is his writing. And sometimes his letters home were fantastic. Here's what he wrote after just a week at Repton:

The chap who takes us in Maths: Major Strickland (Stricker) who is chief of the O.T.C. is terrificly humorous. For instance, he will suddenly turn to you and say, 'Are you a slug, do you leave a long slimey track behind you,' the chap says 'no' and then he says, 'Well you're a fungus, in fact you're wet!' And perhaps he'll make a statement; 'Do you understand,' and then he will repeat it about six times, either getting louder and louder, or softer and softer, in the end developing into a concentrated mumble. He does'nt mind being answered back, but rather likes it; He is also very funny when arguing. For instance, if he cant think of an answer, he'll say, 'Well your . . .' then after the 'your' he will start mumbling, gradually becoming louder and louder, and in the end developing into a low pitched groan. I believe he's half-baked! He's a short man with a face like a field elderberry, and a moustache which closely resembles the African jungle. A voice like a frog, no chest and a pot-belly, no doubt a species of Rumble-hound. Please dont forget the toothpaste and brush.

Love from Roald

Already, I think that Roald wrote just for the fun of it. After all, this piece of writing wasn't for homework or for an exam. It was just to entertain his mother, and whoever else she might show it to. Here is Roald giving his mother some advice:

You seem to have been doing a lot of painting; but when you paint the lav don't paint the seat, leaving it wet and sticky, or some unfortunantely person who has not noticed it, will adhere to it, and unless his bottom is cut off, or unless he chooses to go about with the seat sticking behind him always, he will be doomed to stay where he is . . .

This sounds very typical of the Roald Dahl I knew, and of Roald Dahl's writing – funny, a bit rude, and a bit exaggerated!

Another glimpse of both the masters' odd behaviour and Roald's growing love of exaggerating things comes when he writes:

Mr. Wall is the most bad tempered man on the staff, but otherwise he is very nice. When he looses his temper he goes completly mad, he rushes round the room, tips his desk clean over, with everything on it, kicked all the furniture in the room as hard as he can, and especially his grandfather clock, which is gradually ceasing to exist. He shouts and yells, rushes round the room, and on Wednesday he nearly threw himself out of the window!

Though good marks are still important to him, the school and his mother, he can't resist making a joke of it:

P.S. I got minus 100 marks from our vicious form master last Friday, so I expect I'll be somewhere near bottom at half term.

I think that his mother must have enjoyed his humour and that he tried hard to make her laugh. But I also think that he liked to keep her on the edge of her seat too. Here he is describing the dramatic events when a fire broke out in The Priory:

The flames were enormous and the heat was colossal. The whole place stank of burning . . . and it got in your throat. I coughed all night. However we got to our bedrooms, which the firemen assured us were safe, but to us they looked as though they were being held up by two thin planks. We picked our way gingerly up the stairs (which were black and charcoaly) of course all the electric light had fused long ago. We got into our beds which were brown and nasty and I don't how but I managed to get some sleep. The place looked grimmer than ever by daylight. All the passage was black and in our study absolutely nothing was left.

What I like about this piece of writing is that we can really see and feel what it was like to be there. Roald gives us clear pictures – bedrooms that seem to be 'held up by two thin planks', beds that are 'brown and nasty' and the place looking 'grimmer than ever by daylight'. We also hear about his other senses – we feel the heat, taste the fire in his throat and smell the burning. He takes us on a journey through the scene: we travel with him from watching the fire, up the stairs to the bedrooms, into bed and looking at the study in the daylight. That gives the writing a feeling of movement. There's a changing speed in the story too. We start with lots of busy stuff happening – flames, coughing, firemen – but we end with blackness and nothingness. And he's not afraid to make up a word: *charcoaly*.

Roald entered school poetry competitions and in one poem he wrote a line that I love:

Evening clouds, like frog spawn, spoil the sky.

It turns something very ordinary into something strange and surprising. Not many people would think of comparing evening clouds to frogspawn, but Roald Dahl did. When writers draw our attention to a similarity we may not have noticed before, you can count that as good writing.

He was never afraid of being alone and the other boys noticed that he liked going off in the fields and hills around the school, fishing and collecting birds' eggs. Roald became a hit taking photographs too. Many of his letters were about this or that camera or film. Sometimes he asks his mother to make sure his photos get printed up properly and other times he sent these home, and then his letters are full of explanations about who or what

Photography at Repton

is in which photo. In *Boy*, you can tell that as an adult he was still very proud of how he got to be good at photography, but there's a way that this too is connected to writing. Taking photos carefully, then keeping them and choosing when to show them to people, is like a writer collecting interesting material, storing it up and then deciding when to use it. As you sit about showing people your photos, talking, telling the stories that go with the pictures, you find out what entertains people, what intrigues them, what little exaggerations and jokes you can get away with.

Here he is in that frame of mind in one of his letters:

Playing Fives the other day I knocked a fellows glasses clean off his head with a beautiful sweep of the right arm, because his head unfortunately happened to be in the same place as the ball at that moment. They flew across the floor and shattered into one hundred thousand pieces (which number of course I verified by counting); and so it was one or two days before he could view the world through glass again.

Then there's oodles of information about the biscuits and cakes he likes, and he's especially grateful to his mother for sending him nice ones. This sickly sweet recipe made me think of a very famous chocolate-factory owner:

Yesterday I made some Toffee; dashed good it is too. It cost about 1/10d. 2lbs of sugar. 1/2lb of butter. 2 tins of Nestles condensed milk & some treacle. I have poured it out into greased tin lids, and just cut some out when it is wanted. It is soft of course but dashed good.

Meanwhile, Roald – who was now sixteen years old – had a secret so fabulous that it was surprising he didn't pop with excitement. None of the other boys or masters knew that he had bought a motorbike. He hid it in a barn at a nearby farm and at weekends he would roar through the countryside on his splendid 500cc Ariel. Clad in goggles, helmet, old overcoat and boots, no one recognized him, not even when he rode through Repton, right under the noses of his teachers. I can imagine him leaving school, telling people he's just going for one of his walks . . . making sure no one is following him . . . going to the secret barn . . . climbing on to the bike . . . starting it up . . . hearing the roar of the engine . . . nudging out into the road . . . then speeding past the hedges and trees so that they just become a blur . . . in a world of his own . . . away from school . . . away from everything. It sounds just like one of the stories from his books.

An Ariel 500

It's no surprise that Roald was never made a prefect. A prefect was one of the boys who were in charge, which meant they ruled over the younger ones. The headmaster and housemaster must have seen that Roald wasn't the kind of boy who lived by the rules.

They never knew what he would do next and could see he wasn't someone who would enjoy bossing other boys around. There was even a chance that if they did give him the job of prefect he would do something strange or crazy!

Roald wasn't sad to leave school – quite the opposite, in fact. In *Boy*, he says, 'Without the slightest regret I said goodbye to Repton forever and rode back to Kent on my motorbike.' But, no matter how happy he was to leave Repton, there was one thing that the school gave him and that was the opportunity to develop his writing. Here's something rather wonderful that he wrote while he was there:

Dreams

Once I dreamed of an iceberg. It was a large iceberg which floated on a cold ocean, as if in sleep. A warm mist enveloped all but a thin white line, against which the ocean lapped unceasing. Then, as I lay wondering, the mist slid on, and I saw the iceberg, hard and cold like some great fragment of an icy coast, far away northward.

I awoke, stretched out an arm and pulled up my bed-clothes from the floor. Outside the hoar-frost lay thick on the field, and in the pens the sheep huddled closer for warmth.

Once I dreamed of the tap in our garden. The tap has an old washer, for even Beck, who has never, never used a lever to fit a tyre on the Morris, failed to stop the drip.

And now, as I dreamed, it was dripping as usual, but in the little hole which the water had made, there lay with its leg caught under a smooth brown pebble, a daddy-long-legs.

The drops welled, limpid, on the lip, and fell with a little splash upon the insect below.

I awoke, closed the windows under which I slept and wiped my face on the sheet. Poor daddy-long-legs.

When I dreamed again it was of the Bay of Biscay. All around me I saw the sea, angry as a wounded tiger, sweeping from the North. The waves, like mountains, heaved to and fro, they rose, frowning, paused for a moment then curling savagely, boiled over in a turmoil of green and white – the wounded tiger was showing its teeth.

And all above me hung the wet black clouds, heavy with rain, like airships of paper filled with oil.

I lay on my raft and cursed the Bay of Biscay. I expressed my feelings most aptly in the language I detest, crying with surely as much feeling as Aenias ever cried it: 'Me miserum quanti, mones volucuntur aquarium.' And I began to like Aenias . . .

> *It was the last morning of the term, and in the bedder they had thought of an excellent way of waking me. Four of them were trying to tip me on to the floor; it had not occurred to them that a quicker way of waking me would have been to shake my shoulder; but nothing occurs to anyone on the last morning.*
>
> *Luckily I awoke just before my raft sunk, otherwise I should have discovered to my astonishment that the bottom of the Atlantic was made, not of Planktonic or Forameniferic Oooze but of Repton floorboards, less interesting and harder to fall on.*

What do you think of this piece of writing? I really like it. I like the way it is not only *about* dreaming but also feels dreamy to read.

A short while before he left Repton for good, Roald had passed exams in English, history, maths, science, French and religious education. He knew that when he reached his twenty-fifth birthday he would start to receive a small but regular amount of money which his father had left in trust for him. But that was years away. Some young men in his position joined the army, navy or air force. Others became priests or ministers of the church or missionaries. But none of these jobs appealed to Roald.

His headmaster said that Roald had 'ambition and a real artistic sense . . . If he can master himself, he will be a leader'. By this he meant that he believed that Roald would do very well one day, particularly through writing, music and art, but only if he got himself organized!

I think Roald's headmaster was pretty much spot on, don't you?

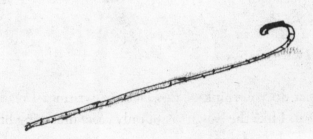

Flying training, Nairobi

The
Man

Roald Dahl, the businessman

Chapter 6

Travels

In July 1934 Roald Dahl's school days had come to an end. He was nearly eighteen years old with his whole future ahead of him. But what was he going to do with his life? He wasn't a writer, not yet. He didn't even seem to think that writing was something he could make into a career.

But there were plenty of things that he loved doing and was good at, such as taking photos, listening to music, bird-spotting, having fun, dreaming up tricks and jokes, travelling, riding his motorbike, inventing gadgets, having adventures, playing cricket and any other game where he could hit a ball with some kind of bat or stick, hanging out with his family – especially his half-brother Louis – and writing, of course. But none of them qualified him for a particular job. And he didn't want to do any more studying, or go to university. This explains why, in his last term at Repton, Roald had applied for – and got – a job with a company that had offices overseas. Because what he really wanted to do was travel the world.

First, Roald had to be trained. And for the next four years, until he was twenty-two, he worked for

Shell Mex House, London

the Shell oil company, sometimes at an oil refinery, but mostly in an office in London. He still lived at home in Bexley. In his spare time, he loved listening to music and reading novels – especially modern American crime novels. He continued taking photos and developed them in a darkroom he'd set up. This was long before digital cameras were invented and developing is a long, slow, painstaking process, with a touch of magic about it. The scene you think you've captured lies hidden and invisible, deep in the heart of the roll of film. Then, when you pour on the right mix of potions and leave them for exactly the right length of time, often in complete darkness or dull red light, the images of those scenes – people's faces, mountains, beaches, cricket teams or whatever – begin to appear on the paper.

Roald started writing short stories and even invented a character called Mr Dippy Dud. It was printed in Shell's company magazine:

Mr Dud is a keen musician, but do not be misled if he's not playing a mouth organ when you see him. He is an equally adept performer on the harmonica, also on the harmonium, euphonium, pandemonium, saxophone, vibraphone, Dictaphone, glockenspiel and catarrh . . . Don't be afraid to tackle anyone you think may be Mr Dud. People who are mistaken for him enter heartily in the fun of the thing, especially town councillors, archdeacons and retired colonels.

At first glance, this may look like a very serious piece of writing, but it's actually a spoof – a piece of writing that pretends to be something that it isn't. Can you see the beginnings of Roald Dahl's writing style? The list of real instruments mixed up with silly ones sounds to me very like the kind of thing that Roald would later write for children.

After four years of footling around in London, Roald's next big adventure began in 1938, when the oil company sent him overseas at last – to East Africa. He travelled there by boat, landing first in Mombasa in Kenya, then going on to the then tiny town of Dar es Salaam in Tanganyika (which is now called Tanzania). He was suddenly surrounded by the wildlife that he'd only read about before, including elephants, leopards, lions and giraffes and snakes. But life in Tanganyika was about to change – in fact, the whole world was about to change – because in September 1939 Britain declared war on Hitler's

Germany. The Second World War had begun.

Roald wrote to the Royal Air Force, saying that he wanted to become a pilot. They agreed to train him. And then he wrote to his mother, telling her how it would be 'very good fun', much better than being in the army, 'marching about in the heat from one place to another', and, what's more, they would teach him how to fly aeroplanes.

Roald Dahl loved gadgets, machines and speed. He loved FUN. He loved spending time on his own – whether that was on his motorbike, in the darkroom, listening to music or aboard a rickety boat on rough seas in Norway. He also seems to have liked the idea of danger. He had no idea just how scary and awful the war was going to be, nor what a terrible loss of life there would be, especially among these young pilots.

So Roald left Dar es Salaam and went to Nairobi in Kenya, where the RAF were going to teach him to fly . . . and immediately hit a big problem. Or rather, a tall problem. With a height of six feet and six inches – or two metres – Roald was too tall to fit into a fighter-plane.

The planes were Tiger Moths, and, compared to modern planes, these aircraft were tiny, weak, fragile things. If ever you look at one in a museum or on the Internet, you'll see that some of them didn't even have canopies – the pilots were exposed to the wind. In most planes there was a kind of windscreen, like on an open-topped car, which protected their faces a little. But Roald's head was higher than the windscreen. This meant that, once he had got up speed and was flying, he could hardly breathe. He got round it, though. He tied a thin cotton cloth over his nose and mouth to stop himself from choking.

Soon he was loving it. He wrote to his mother, 'I've never enjoyed myself so much . . .' Terrible things were happening far, far away in Poland and France, but Roald was like a tourist, flying over the beautiful savannah of Kenya and the Great Rift Valley, amazed by the breathtaking scenes of beauty. In his little plane, he could skim along just above the ground, watching herds of giraffes and wildebeest. He was seeing something that only a handful of people had ever seen. If you are a writer, you often want to feel that you're one of the few to have seen, heard or experienced something, so that when you write you can imagine you're bringing your readers the news. People who got to know Roald Dahl better than I did said the feeling that he was a person who had some news was something he liked very much. He liked having some kind of secret knowledge that he could share with you, or shock you with.

Then things started getting a bit more serious. Roald and his fellow trainee pilots – there were sixteen of them – travelled to Uganda, then on to Cairo and into Iraq. They were being prepared to fight in the hot, dry lands of North Africa, where the war was now being fought too. It was in Iraq that Roald finished his training.

In the mornings, he and the other pilots flew Hawker Harts and Audaxes – planes that were armed with bombs and machine guns. This was not just learning how to fly. This was training for  war, learning how to kill. But in the afternoons they could relax, sometimes wandering about the ancient city of Baghdad. It was unbelievably hot, up to 50°C. Daily life was full of flies, sandstorms, scorpions and snakes.

After a few months, Roald Dahl was made a pilot officer, passing his tests with 'Special Distinction'. Out of forty pilots, he came third, and the other two men had already known how to fly before the war. A report said that he had exceptional flying ability. He could swoop and swerve and dive and climb and do the scariest manoeuvre of them all – the loop-the-loop. He was proud to wear his RAF flying badge.

It was now September 1940. Roald had just turned twenty-four years old and what took place next would affect him for the rest of his life. It happened when he was flying a Gloster Gladiator, a little plane that he was taking from the Suez Canal to a secret location in the North African desert. He landed near Alexandria in Egypt on a tiny runway where there were just a few tents and other aeroplanes. He needed more fuel, he was tired and it was getting late. He asked the commanding officer for some directions. The officer phoned ahead and then asked Roald for his map, pointing to a spot in the middle of the desert. Roald was concerned that when he arrived it would be too dark to see and that the runway would be hidden with camouflage.

'You can't miss it,' the officer told him.

But after a while Roald started to get worried. There he was, up in the sky, above the desert. It was getting dark. The wind was blowing the sand about. Below him were rocks, sand, little valleys and humps in the ground – mile after mile after mile, stretching away into the distance. He looked hard for a runway, some tents or other aeroplanes, but he couldn't see a thing. Nothing at all.

And now he was running out of fuel. He didn't even have enough to get him back to Alexandria. What could he do? What would you do?

Roald decided to take a chance. He thought he would be able to land the plane somewhere flat. So he flew towards the ground, slowed down and hoped for the best. But it was no good. The plane hit a rock, dived nose-first into the ground and smashed up. Inside, tangled among the wreckage, was Roald.

His head had crashed against the plane. The fuel then caught light and the aircraft burst into flames. Meanwhile, the guns and bullets on board were whizzing and zinging in all directions. Roald could easily have been hit by one of them.

This is how the authorities wrote about it in the official report:

Pilot Officer Dahl was ferrying an aircraft from No. 102 Maintenance Unit to this unit, but unfortunately not being used to flying aircraft over the desert he made a forced landing two miles west of Mersah Matruh. He made an unsuccessful forced landing and the aircraft burst into flames. The pilot was badly burned and he was conveyed to an Army Field Ambulance station.

Luckily Roald's plane was spotted coming down and two soldiers from a nearby base came out to find him. He was so badly smashed up and burned, and the plane was so badly damaged, that at first they didn't even know he was in the RAF. They took him back to the base, where the army doctors thought he was an Italian pilot – in other words, the enemy! When they realized Roald was in the RAF, they sent him on to the Anglo-Swiss hospital in Alexandria. There the doctors and nurses got to work straight away, treating his burns, his concussion and something that would hurt him for the rest of his life – his back.

At first the doctors thought he might have been permanently blinded in the crash. So did Roald. For several weeks, he couldn't see. He was dizzy and sick and faded in and out of consciousness. Later, when he was better, Roald wrote a short story called 'Beware of the Dog'. I wonder if he was describing what it felt like in those early days after his crash.

The whole world was white and there was nothing in it. It was so white that sometimes it looked black, and after a time it was either white or black, but mostly it was white. He watched it as it turned from white to black, then back to white again, and the white stayed a long time, but the black lasted only a few seconds. He got into the habit of going to sleep during the white periods, of waking up just in time to see the world when it was black. The black was very quick. Sometimes it was only a flash, a flash of black lightning. The white was slow, and in the slowness of it, he always dozed off.

If you look at the first three sentences again, you'll see that he mentions the word 'white' seven times! When we write, we can say something like 'for a lot of the time the world looked white' and leave it at that. Or we can find ways of saying that same thing by repeating a word. This way, the words don't just say what's happening, they start to sound and feel just like the way a person is thinking. The way you write imitates your thoughts. I think it's really interesting that one of the ways Roald became a writer was through trying to write about one of the most awful experiences he ever went through.

So, Roald lay in bed in a strange, dreamlike state, slowly on the mend. But in the middle of it all he heard some news from back home. His mother's house in Bexley had been bombed. His mother and sisters were all right. That was good. But he had lost his precious camera, photos and notebooks. And that wasn't so good. The war was starting to affect everyone and everything Roald knew and loved.

After two months, several operations and hundreds of hours' sleep, Roald started to feel better. His face was remodelled by a plastic surgeon who – as Roald told his mother – 'pulled my nose out of the back of my head and shaped it'. He said that the nose looked 'just as before except that it's a little bent about'. Like in the letters he sent from school, Roald again seemed to be trying to stop his mother from worrying too much about her only son.

After a few more months, he was feeling better still. And the RAF agreed that he was fit and well . . . so they sent him back to the war.

Roald Dahl's Hurricane

Roald Dahl's Jobs

The Businessman

'I enjoyed it, I really did. I began to realize how simple life could be if one had a regular routine to follow with fixed hours and a fixed salary and very little original thinking. The life of a writer is absolute hell compared with the life of a businessman.'

The Fighter Pilot

'I don't think any fighter pilot has ever managed to convey what it is like to be up there in a long-lasting dog-fight . . . It was truly the most breathless and the most exhilarating time I have ever had in my life. I caught glimpses of planes with black smoke pouring from their engines. I saw planes with pieces of metal flying off their fuselages . . . The sky was so full of aircraft that half my time was spent in actually avoiding collisions.'

The Spy

His proper title was Assistant Air Attaché, but REALLY Roald Dahl was a spy. This must have come in very handy indeed when he was writing the screenplay for the James Bond film – *You Only Live Twice*.

The Toilet-seat Warmer!

It's true. This was Roald's job when he was at school. The toilets were in an unheated outhouse and in winter he had to wipe the frost off the toilet seat and then warm up the seat for one of the Boazers (prefects).

The Writer

Do you think this was Roald's favourite job of all? I do.

Roald Dahl's passport

Chapter 7

War Hero and Spy

It was March 1941. Roald was twenty-five and an RAF pilot once more, who soared through the sky in a Mark I Hurricane, a modern, fast-flying machine, doing his bit to win the war against Germany and her allies.

The Battle of Britain, a battle fought in the skies in 1940 between the Germans and the British, helped to glamorize all RAF pilots, no matter where they flew. This is partly because the pilots did what very few people in the 1940s had experienced: flying fast and high. Another reason – and it's a sad and awful reason – is that so many of these very young men were shot down in their planes and killed. So, just being alive meant that there was something almost magical about them. If they had survived the many dangers of flying in wartime, surely they could survive anything?

When I was a boy, we imitated these pilots with our toy planes, looping the loop and making ack-ack-ack noises as we shot down the imaginary enemy. In the movies we watched, the men were always handsome, calm and brave. And women always fell in love with them. At school, if one of our teachers had been in the RAF during the war, we knew that he'd been to places and seen things that were more incredible than we could imagine. We also knew that he must be full of stories, just like those in our adventure books and comics, where the pilot sat in his cockpit, his helmet on, enemy planes in the sky behind him, shouting out to his tail gunner, 'Let him have it, Binky!' And then the air would be full of zigzag lines and noises like 'BLAM! BLAM! BLAM!' and the next picture would show a plume of smoke in the sky.

Whether he liked it or not, Roald became one of these hero-like characters. Although he didn't fly in the Battle of Britain itself, he and his fellow pilots – all members of 80 Squadron – fought a series of brave air battles, mostly above Greece. At the time, he wrote about what was happening in letters to his mother and to his friends.

Of all the shocking things that happened, death affected him the most – the deaths of his young friends and the deaths of the young men he had to kill. His way of coping was by trying to be indifferent, or not caring. Whether he managed this or not, I don't know. Perhaps he was very good at pretending that he didn't care. But later in life, as he wrote more and more, at least some of that indifference – real or otherwise – vanished. He had to care about his characters – Matilda, Danny, Sophie and the rest – so that when we read about them in his books we care about them too. On the other hand, he wrote *Dirty Beasts* and *Revolting Rhymes* and one of the reasons why those poems are so funny is that people die or do horrible things to each other in ways that don't really seem to matter. Those poems seem to me to almost laugh at death. Perhaps this is what Roald Dahl learned to do in the midst of all that sadness and loss when he was a pilot during the war. What do you think?

Roald's crash had left him with terrible headaches and, after a year of active service, these headaches grew so bad that he had to be sent home. He had been away from his mother and his sisters for three years. After everything he and they had been through, their reunion must have been a very emotional experience. Many years later, when he was reading aloud the last chapter of his second autobiography, *Going Solo*, to an audience at the National Theatre in London, his daughter Ophelia saw him crying. It seems as if that sadness still remained many years later.

What was left of Roald's old house had been taken over by the British Army. (As the country was at war, the army could do that at any time.) His new home was now a strange, much smaller, older house in a little village called Ludgershall in Buckinghamshire and it was here that he planned to spend time recovering from the war . . . except, he couldn't do that. Just because the RAF had sent Roald back to England didn't mean that they were finished with him. Not yet. There were plenty of jobs on the ground for him, like helping the RAF to find and train more pilots. But this wasn't really what Roald wanted to do.

What happened next was like something out of a James Bond movie. A member of parliament took Roald out for a meal in a tiny, very posh gentlemen's club. It was a strange and secretive meeting in which Roald was offered a job at the British Embassy in Washington, USA. He would be called an Assistant Air Attaché. This hush-hush job offer must have been very exciting for someone like Roald, who loved tricks, plots and plans. But what would he actually be doing?

In March 1942 the USA had only just joined in the war. Most people in Britain had desperately wanted such a big, rich and powerful nation to become involved because they would be able to supply millions of soldiers, planes, boats and tanks. But the Americans were still very divided about the war. Some had always thought that they should join in, while others thought that they definitely shouldn't.

The British government, headed by Winston Churchill, decided that they needed some of their own people in the USA, people whose role would be to keep America on Britain's side in the war. And it was Roald's job to encourage very powerful people in the American government to support Britain, reminding them what the RAF was doing and making sure that stories showing what a terrible time the British people were having got into the American newspapers.

It would also be Roald's job to report back to Churchill and his ministers on the mood of the country – whether the Americans were more or less keen to support Britain, whether there was any gossip from people in high places that Britain needed to know about.

Roald's new job looked like a lot of fun – dinner parties, tennis matches, barbecues, late-night chats with newspaper reporters and long conversations about going up in planes and being brave. But, underneath the glitz and the socializing, it was really all about collecting and sending out information. This job has a name: intelligence. And the fantastically exciting word for it is 'spying'. Roald Dahl had become a spy. He would work for the British government by spying on the USA, a country that was, to a large extent, friends with Britain.

So off he went. He travelled by train to Glasgow in Scotland, where he boarded a ship and headed off across the Atlantic Ocean to Canada. Then he went by train from Montreal to Washington, DC, to stay in the Willard Hotel until he found an apartment.

✳

And that's how Roald added something else to the amazing list that people tend to put after his name – you know the sort of thing: 'Roald Dahl, world-famous bestselling writer, war hero and spy . . .'

Roald was about to begin the next chapter in his life, in a place where things were very different from what he was used to. And, talking of chapters, it really does seem that Roald Dahl was someone whose life was a series of wildly different chapters. It was as if he finished one adventure and then started on another straight away, in a new place and with new people. I don't know if that's something he created for himself or if life just kept happening to him that way. What do you think?

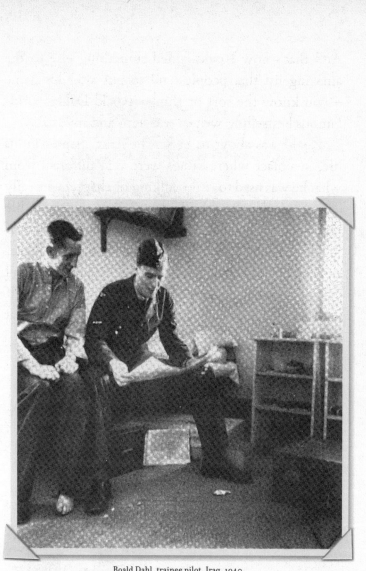

Roald Dahl, trainee pilot, Iraq, 1940

Roald Dahl in his writing hut

The
Writer

Roald Dahl in the RAF

Chapter 8

Gremlins

I once watched a documentary that claimed polar bears survive because they are endlessly curious. It showed a polar bear coming up to a camera and sniffing it and poking it. I think writers are a bit like polar bears. They are forever sniffing out things, listening and remembering, so that they can turn them into stories, which they sell and that helps them make a living, which means that they survive too!

On the way to his top-secret job in North America, Roald met someone called Douglas Bisgood, a wounded pilot like him. Douglas had fought in the Battle of Britain and before that he had been a racing-car driver. As the two men headed across the Atlantic, they joked and gossiped together.

During the war, RAF pilots became famous for inventing their own slang – special words and ways of saying things. For example, a plane was a 'crate' and a crash was a 'prang'. Put that together and they might say, 'Did you hear about Lofty? He pranged his crate . . .' These pilots, who were living life on the edge, never knowing which flight might be their last, also seemed to have invented their own folklore. They made up stories about little mischievous imp-like creatures who lived in and around the planes, often making the aircraft go horribly wrong but sometimes protecting the pilots. They called them 'gremlins'.

For someone on the verge of becoming a writer, this sort of thing is treasure! Roald's mother had once filled his young head with stories of the trolls and giants of Norwegian folklore. Now, on the deck of the SS *Batori*, Roald and Douglas swapped folklore and made up new stories about gremlins. Sounds like good fun to me.

In Washington, Roald found himself far away from the dangerous world of the fighter pilot and far away from hungry, bombed-out, war-torn London. There were massive amounts of food and drink, and lots of parties. He had oodles of time to listen to his beloved music. All he had to do was give speeches about the great work that the RAF was doing and keep his ear to the ground. Roald had to play the part of a handsome, brave, British chap who had done his best to win the war. It wasn't difficult, because he was and he had.

Meanwhile, inside his head, the gremlins were stirring. And Roald couldn't keep them to himself. He wrote to a magazine about his idea:

> *'The gremlins comprise a very real and considerable part of the conversation of every RAF pilot in the world. Every*

This is the Roald Dahl I recognize – the Roald Dahl who writes about amazing, funny, odd creatures, making it seem as if they're part of everyday life and – guess what – doing something rude!

Next, he got down to writing an actual story. He called the gremlins' wives 'Fifinellas' and their children 'Widgets' or 'Flipperty-Gibbets'. They lived in a 'beautiful green wood far up in the North. They could walk up and down trees in their special suction boots'. Then horrible humans came and chopped down their trees so that they could build factories and roads and airports. So the gremlins took revenge! They attached themselves to planes and caused accidents. They moved mountains so that the planes would fly straight into them. And they made tiny holes in the side of a plane flown by a pilot called Gus. But Gus was wily and inventive. He fed the gremlins postage stamps and played tricks on them. And, in the end, they become friends.

Roald had created a story – a good story. But

what was he to do with it? How could he turn it into a book?

First, believe it or not, he had to show the story to his bosses for their approval because he was still working for the RAF and everything he did, said and wrote belonged to them. Then he sent it to a magazine where it was published for the first time.

Most writers will tell you that they had a lucky break. Perhaps someone sitting at a desk or next to them on a train or at a party was just the right person at just the right time to help. And perhaps this someone not only was able to see something good in the writing but was also in a job where they could help the story to get out there. For Roald, this someone was a friend who knew the famous film-maker Walt Disney. Walt Disney read Roald's gremlin story and cabled back a message saying that he was interested in turning it into a movie.

WOW. How cool is that!

I don't know what Roald did when he heard this. I like to think that he jumped up and down, ran round the block, rang his mother and sisters in England and threw a party. But if he did, he kept it quiet. He was pleased. But he didn't let himself get carried away.

Roald was invited to Hollywood. He took leave from his job and, before he knew it, he was in the most glamorous place on earth, meeting top movie stars, like the great silent-movie actor Charlie Chaplin.

They thought Roald was funny and cute and quite extraordinary, with a really cool accent. They'd read his story. And they loved it. It wasn't long before Disney 'shot a test reel' – that's a try-out bit of film.

But, although *The Gremlins* had become his very first book and it was going to be a Walt Disney movie, Roald wasn't happy. He didn't particularly like the Disney drawings or the toy gremlins you could buy in the shops. And he found out that Walt Disney himself was worrying whether the time had passed for this kind of film about pilots in the war. Eventually, Disney gave up on the project and told Roald that he wasn't going to finish the movie. That was it. The End.

Except it wasn't The End.

Roald Dahl was nearly twenty-seven years old and now ready to become a great writer. All he needed was a place to write, time to write and enough reasons to go on writing.

It was really The Beginning . . .

Things you might **not** know

1. His favourite sound was the piano.

2. His favourite TV programme was the News.

3. His most frightening
   moment was in his
   Hurricane plane,
   1941, RAF.

4. If he had not
   been a writer, he
   would have been
   a doctor.

5. He owned a hundred budgerigars.

6. His favourite smell was frying bacon.

7. He loathed Christmas.

8. He loved Easter.

9. In the churchyard at Great
   Missenden, GIANT
   footprints lead to
   his grave.

10. He liked to play Scrabble, but wasn't very good at
    it because of his ~~apalling~~ ~~appaling~~ terrible spelling!

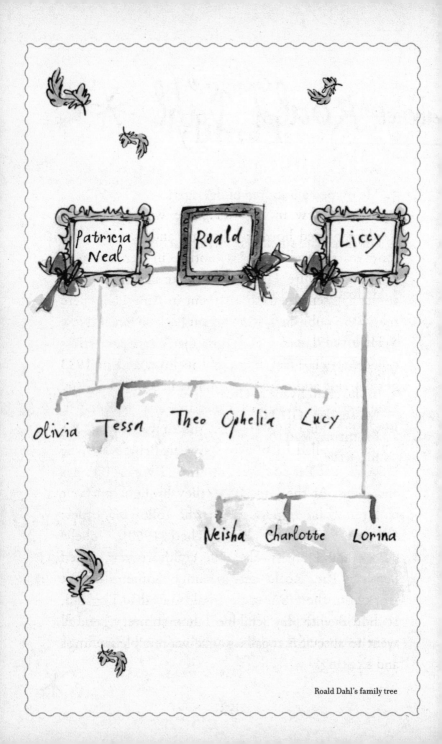

Roald Dahl's family tree

Chapter 9

Family

In 1946, a few months after the war had ended, Roald returned home to England and, for the next four years, lived with his mother in her house in Buckinghamshire. He began to write short stories for adults and sent them to his agent in America, where they were published. Roald went back to live in New York in 1951 and a year later met a famous actress called Patricia Neal. They fell in love, and in 1953 got married and returned to England to live in Gispy House near to Roald's mother in Great Missenden. But they didn't live there all the time. Instead, the couple travelled to and fro between Britain and the USA so that Pat could act in films, TV programmes and plays. At the same time, they brought up their children, who came along in the following order: Olivia (1955), Tessa (1957), Theo (1960), Ophelia (1964) and Lucy (1965). The childcare was shared between Pat, Roald and a nanny. Sometimes, Pat worked in the USA while Roald stayed in England, at home with the children. Sometimes, they all went to the USA together. Life was very glamorous and exciting.

Meanwhile, Roald was still writing stories for adults. They were full of strange and mysterious goings-on, and characters with nasty or odd ways of thinking and behaving. He loved that kind of fiction, and so did the many Roald Dahl fans who gobbled it up. So, if he was doing well with this type of story, why did he begin writing for children instead? I think that spending so much time around his own children as they grew up might be one of the reasons why Roald became a children's writer.

In his notebook Roald began to jot down ideas and plots for children's stories. On one occasion he stood looking at the fruit in his garden. Why, he wondered, did the apples and pears in his garden stop growing? Why didn't they just go on and on and on growing? And what if, instead of apples or pears, it was a peach? This was how *James and the Giant Peach* started out and in 1961 it became the first of his books for children to be published.

It would be wonderful to imagine

that Roald Dahl's life went on in a magical storybook way, but three tragic events then took place that would have a huge effect on him.

When Theo was four months old, his pram was hit by a taxi in New York City. He suffered terrible head injuries and had to be nursed carefully for years. But, despite many complications, he survived. Roald became very involved with his son's treatment. He worked with a brilliant toymaker and a surgeon to invent a tiny device that would drain the fluid that sometimes builds up after such accidents out of a patient's brain. This became known as the Dahl–Wade–Till valve. Although it was never used on Theo, the valve was used to treat nearly three thousand children all over the world. Somehow, and without any proper training in science or technology, Roald Dahl had become a great inventor.

Roald continued to look after the children when Pat was away filming, as well as working on his next story for children, *Charlie and the Chocolate Factory*. But then in 1962 a second tragedy occurred. Olivia died from complications from measles – she was just seven years old. This was exactly the same age that Roald's sister Astri had been when she died. Perhaps that helped him, perhaps not. It's certainly something he thought about, as he mentions the coincidence of ages in *Boy*.

I can see some of this in close focus. I had a son who

died and the same thing had happened to my father too. He had a son who died before I was born. I've a funny feeling that both Roald and I coped with all the sadness and rage and disbelief in a similar fashion. Roald tried very hard to understand how and why Olivia died. He tried to be scientific about it, writing down in a calm, factual manner the exact sequence of events that led to her death. Afterwards, he was determined to make sure that other children received the measles vaccine.

Eventually, though, the tragedies were too much for Roald and for a long time he was very, very depressed. One way he and Pat found some hope was by helping other children through charity work.

Then the third tragedy hit: Pat became very seriously ill. She suffered a huge stroke. A stroke can mean different things to different people, depending on how severe it is. Some might find that they stop being able to use parts of their body. They might find that they can't speak or walk properly. Pat's stroke looked like it might be one of the worst.

But Roald wasn't going to be beaten. He decided to get Pat better, introducing what looked to some like a military regime – a round of exercises and activity that could never for one day, one hour, one moment stop. Roald was in charge. He gave the orders and it was Pat's job to obey them. This, Roald said, was the only way she could get better.

It sounds like a strange fairy tale, but amazingly and incredibly she did get better. Patricia Neal even went back to acting. It's such a fascinating story that a film was made about it!

Meanwhile, there were four children who needed to be looked after. Friends of the children tell stories about how amazing Roald seemed to them. Here was this incredibly tall, gangly man who was full of hobbies and stories. He was always tinkering about with bits of old furniture, listening to music, talking about art or famous people he knew. And he did unbelievably naughty things. In a restaurant, he might ask what the 'special' was. Then, when the waiter told him, he would say in a loud voice so that the whole restaurant could hear, 'Don't ever get the "special", it's probably last night's leftovers. They only tell you it's the "special" so that they can get rid of it!'

And there was always the chocolate. From his schooldays at Repton, which wasn't far from the Cadbury's factory at Bournville, Roald loved chocolate. So he had a box at the main table in the house that was always packed full of chocolate bars. After every meal, the box was circulated around the table and he would even give a few Smarties to his beloved dog Chopper.

And, talking of chocolate, *Charlie and the Chocolate Factory* was to become his most famous book of all. In America there were plans to turn it into a film. Suddenly everyone was talking about Roald Dahl – but unfortunately not in a good way. Back then, in the 1960s, American Civil Rights activists were trying to make sure black people and white people were treated equally. Many thought that the Oompa-Loompas made black people sound silly, undignified and inferior. Some organizations said that no way should a film version of this book be made. Roald agreed to turn the Oompa-Loompas into white characters, and the film – under the slightly different title of *Willy Wonka and the Chocolate Factory* – went into production.

I don't think Roald Dahl invented the Oompa-Loompas to cause offence. He was not the type of person who would do things like that. But I do think

that perhaps he hadn't realized how certain words, pictures, images and ways of saying things suggest to children that some people are superior and some inferior.

None of this was to stop Roald Dahl from writing and telling stories. Sometimes, he would wake the children – and any of their friends who were staying for a sleepover – and take them  for midnight walks down the lane to the arch under the railway, tell them a scary story or two and then march them back to bed.

Then, instead of going to work, like most of the other dads nearby seemed to do, he either pottered about in the house or walked up the garden to his special hut, to write.

By the end of the 1970s Roald had published five more books for children, which were *The Magic Finger*, *Fantastic Mr Fox*, *Charlie and the Great Glass Elevator*, *Danny the Champion of the World* and *The Enormous Crocodile*. At this point in time, Roald and Pat's life together was drifting apart and in 1983 they were divorced. Later that year Roald married

Felicity, who is usually called Liccy (pronounced 'Lissy'). Roald's new wife had three children of her own, so now there were seven children.

In 1977 Roald became a grandfather too. His daughter Tessa had a baby girl: Sophie. She heard the early versions of *The BFG* and the Sophie in the book is named after her. One of the ways Roald got his granddaughter interested in the idea of a big friendly giant who collects dreams was first to tell her the story and then, at night, to climb up a ladder and appear at her bedroom window, just like the BFG!

Can you imagine lying in bed upstairs, when suddenly you see your granddad looking through the window . . . ?

People who visited the Dahl house at this time spoke of how full of people it always seemed to be. It was rowdy and rude, with lots of jokes and noise and music. It rather looks as if Roald had made another Dahl gang, a bit like the family he grew up in.

By the 1980s Roald was world-famous. Millions of people were reading his books, watching his TV programmes and seeing films that he had been involved with. Many people knew that he was often in pain because of his injuries from the plane crash. And some people knew that inside must be hidden away the many things that made him sad.

I once saw him at a big book festival organized by his publisher Puffin Books. It was wonderful to watch hundreds, probably thousands of children trying to get into a hall to hear him read from his latest book. I sneaked in and realized that everyone was listening. And I remember thinking that there was something both sad and funny about his eyebrows. If you lift up your eyebrows, you can do it in a way that makes people laugh, because you look so surprised. And you can also do it in a way that looks sad, as if life has taken you by surprise in a not-very-nice way . . . I remember thinking that Roald Dahl's face and his eyebrows were like this.

Each time a new book came out there was a
WHOOP across the world. Children loved them.
A few days later, they would be telling each other
about the incredible things they'd read – about Bruce
Bogtrotter and the enormous chocolate cake from
Matilda or maybe the amazing whizzpopping scene in
front of . . . no . . . surely not . . . the Queen? Not any
old imaginary queen, but the real Queen. No way!
Yes! Really? Yes!!

Ask any writer what it's like when people are reading and enjoying and talking about your book and they will probably reply that it's one of the best feelings in the world. I certainly think so. And I'm sure Roald Dahl felt the same.

Roald Dahl in his writing hut

Chapter 10

How He Wrote Books

How did Roald Dahl go about writing such fabulously original and funny – and really quite rude – books, one after another?

First, he always did things in the same way. For most of his life, Roald liked writing with a yellow pencil called a Dixon Ticonderoga 1388-2 5/10, medium. (Try saying that quickly!) He wrote on American yellow legal pads, which were sent to him from New York City. It may come as no surprise to learn that yellow was his favourite colour.

Next, he had a special place where he wrote. He and a builder friend built a little brick hut in his garden in Great Missenden. Inside he put things that he liked and he arranged his chair – which had a hole cut in just the right place so that it didn't press on his injured back – to be in the perfect spot, with a special board across the arms of the chair for him to rest his paper on.

When he was writing a book, Roald would walk through the garden to his hut, close the door and no one was allowed to disturb him. Well, that's how it was supposed to be, but you know better than me what children are like! Yes, they would occasionally pop in and out but I imagine the only creatures most likely to see Roald Dahl at work were the cows in the next-door field. If they had peeped through the window, they would have seen Roald scribbling away with his pencil on his yellow paper. Usually, he did his writing only in the morning and in the late afternoon, which would leave him free to do all the other business and fun things during the rest of the day.

Inside his hut, Roald went into a kind of trance. He concentrated so hard that he could whisk himself away to all sorts of different places in his mind – visiting scenes and people and things, both real and

imaginary. It was here that he came up with plots and plans and schemes – the wicked tricks that happen so often in his stories. He had a notebook to capture his ideas and whenever he thought of something, he scribbled it down. Then, later, if he was wondering what to write next, he could comb through his notebook, looking for ideas.

Most writers I know have notebooks. I do. I sometimes think that I have a notebook because I'm afraid that I'll forget things. That's not such a crazy idea, because writing was invented as a way of remembering things. And maybe that's what Roald was doing – trying to hang on to his thoughts and memories. He was always on the lookout for stuff that would surprise his readers, even if it was shocking or disgusting. Sometimes, he was just capturing a bit of language. I imagine that he thought something like this: *I like that . . . I like the way it sounds . . . I like the image it conjures up in my mind . . . I mustn't forget that . . . I'll put that in my ideas book because it might come in handy when I'm trying to describe someone in a story*. I can't tell you if Roald really thought that, but I can tell you that I do.

Like a lot of writers, when Roald was in the middle of writing a book he could be quite twitchy and irritable. Why? To me, it's because the book feels like unfinished business. I am nervous about whether it will work out or not. I worry if I get stuck or if

I think that this book is not turning out as well as the last book. Half of me wants to show the book to other people, the other half thinks that if I show it to someone else, they'll blow away the magic that's making the book happen in the first place or they'll suggest something that will send the story off in totally the wrong direction.

After he'd finished a book and sent it off to the publisher, instead of dancing with relief, Roald would be worried. Sometimes he wondered if he would ever write anything again, and the thought of this made him grumpy. But, as we know, he did go on and on writing, and with the books came stupendous success.

I'm guessing that you've read a few of them (see the whole list on page 160) and I'm also guessing that you have favourite scenes, favourite people and also characters you most like to hate and despise. I hope so, because I think that's part of the fun in reading. But was Roald Dahl trying to say something to us with all with these books?

In *Matilda*, Roald seems to be saying over and over again, 'Don't forget to read books!' But there's a LOT more going on. He paints a picture of a school that is so horrible and a teacher who is so lovely that it's almost as if he's dreaming of the perfect school – one where every teacher is as nice and as kind to children as Miss Honey. And what about Matilda's parents? Is he saying that children deserve better parents than these and that if they don't have them, and if they read and read and read, they can get themselves a better life?

And then there's *Danny the Champion of the World*. I like this book a lot. It's a story about people who don't have very much and people who have too much. There's a father and son who get on really well and together they play an amazing trick that . . . well, I couldn't possibly say. If you've read the book, you'll KNOW. If you haven't, go and find a copy at once. You won't be disappointed, I promise. But despite  this fabulous, amazing plot that I'm *not* going to tell you about, Roald wrote something else that he would repeat over and over again. Danny's dad was 'sparky' and Roald said that parents should always try to be sparky. What do you think he meant?

When *The Twits* and *George's Marvellous Medicine* and *The Witches* came out, some people started to wonder just how beastly Roald Dahl could get. Were all his books going to be full of incurably horrible characters? And was destroying them the only way to stop them being so despicable? Some people said that too many of these nasty people were women.

Once again, Roald found himself arguing with his critics. He told them that in his books he had horrible women and nice women. And hadn't all stories for children always been like this? In particular, some critics picked out the passage at the beginning of *The Witches* where he says that any woman you meet could turn out to be a witch. Was he trying to make children suspicious of women?

Look at Grandmamma in *The Witches*, he and his defenders said. Look at Sophie in *The BFG*. They were both clever, tender female characters. And he would go on to write about Matilda and Miss Honey in *Matilda* too.

Now, I'll let you into a secret. Did you know that writers don't always get a story right the first time round? It's true. They might try out a storyline and if they or the people who help make the books (the agents, editors and publishers) don't think that the storyline works, they try another one. It's a bit like going to a clothes shop, trying on an outfit, looking in the mirror, deciding if you like what you're wearing, listening to what other people think and then trying on something else. It rarely comes out right the first time. A book is really the end of a long and winding road. Roald wrote several drafts and it often took him over a year to finish a whole story.

Here are some of the storylines that Roald tried out and then scrapped. Which do you prefer – the early storyline or the version that made it into a book?

James and the Giant Peach

The original cast list starred a Hairy-Green Caterpillar and an Earwig. But there was no Old-Green-Grasshopper, no Miss Spider and no Glow-worm either.

The Enormous Crocodile

The crocodile is whirled up into the sky by Trunky the elephant, but instead of hitting the sun he falls safely to earth.

The Twits

Mr and Mrs Twit are stuck upside-down forever.

George's Marvellous Medicine

At the end of the book, Grandma is still incredibly tall.

The Witches

Bruno the mouse became a spy for the British government.

Matilda

Instead of being good, Matilda was the wickedest child in the world. Meanwhile, her parents were really nice and long-suffering. Miss Honey didn't even exist. And there was no Miss Trunchbull either. Instead, there was a teacher called Miss Hayes, who loved betting on horses. Matilda used her special powers to make sure that the horse she wanted to win was first past the post. And that was what kept her from going to prison! In the end this really dreadful Matilda died in a car crash. Oh dear.

Looking at some of Roald's early drafts reminds me that he tried very, very, very hard indeed to make you laugh, make you surprised, make you amazed. Perhaps you think that writing is pretty easy – all you have to do is sit on your backside scribbling a few words down. Well, I'm not going to say it's the hardest thing in the world to do. But I will say that Roald Dahl was a writer who tried hard, day after day after day, to make the stories work. If you really like his books – perhaps love them – then that's because of this hard work. You can't see the hard work, because reading is about fun and enjoyment and interest. And that is part of the magic of writing.

What is it about the way Roald Dahl wrote that makes his books such fun? I think there are LOTS of things he does to entertain his  readers. You might think of totally different things. But that's what is so splendid about books – there are no right answers. Everyone is allowed to have their own ideas about what is and what isn't GREAT.

First, let's peek inside the pages of *Matilda*. Here, the terrible Miss Trunchbull is confronting poor Bruce Bogtrotter:

His plump flabby face had turned grey with fearful apprehension. His stockings hung about his ankles.

'This clot,' boomed the Headmistress, pointing the riding-crop at him like a rapier, 'this black-head, this foul carbuncle, this poisonous pustule that you see before you is none other than a disgusting criminal, a denizen of the underworld, a member of the Mafia!'

'Who, me?' Bruce Bogtrotter said, looking genuinely puzzled.

'A thief!' the Trunchbull screamed. 'A crook! A pirate! A brigand! A rustler!'

'Steady on,' the boy said, 'I mean, dash it all, Headmistress.'

'Do you deny it, you miserable little gumboil? Do you plead not guilty?'

'I don't know what you're talking about,' the boy said, more puzzled than ever.

I love all the different names Miss Trunchbull calls Bruce Bogtrotter. But in real life, people don't usually talk like this. Try it. Pretend you're really angry about something or somebody and make a list of insults. It's actually quite hard. But it's very entertaining. This kind of writing is called exaggeration or hyperbole, which is pronounced 'high-per-bolly' – a word that

I'm sure Roald would have loved.

Flip back a few pages to the very beginning of *Matilda*.

It's a funny thing about mothers and fathers. Even when their own child is the most disgusting little blister you could ever imagine, they still think that he or she is wonderful. Some parents go further. They become so blinded by adoration they manage to convince themselves their child has qualities of genius.

Well, there is nothing very wrong with all this. It's the way of the world. It is only when the parents begin telling us about the brilliance of their revolting offspring, that we start shouting, 'Bring us a basin! We're going to be sick!'

A fun thing to do with writing like this is to think about who's speaking. Is it Roald Dahl? Maybe . . . except Matilda is fiction and Roald was absolutely real. In most storybooks, the person telling the story is usually someone pretending to be the author – as if it's a diary or a memoire – or a kind of invisible storyteller who isn't a character, just someone who can magically tell us what's happening.

One of the really intriguing things about Roald

Dahl's books is that he liked to say Roald-Dahl-ish things and do the invisible-storytelling thing, sometimes in the same book, sometimes on the same page. What's more, the Roald-Dahl-ish things are often rude, funny, amazing or totally outrageous.

In this extract, it sounds as if Roald is in the same room, just chatting. It's actually quite hard to write like that, because you have to forget all the stuff you've been told about making sentences long and interesting, with loads of describing words and plenty of connectives – like 'but' and 'and' and 'because' – to join them all together. Instead, you have to make the sentences short and snappy, with very few connectives, because that's how most of us speak when we're just chatting to each other. Look at the very first sentence: 'It's a funny thing about mothers and fathers.' There's no introduction to that sentence. It's almost as if Roald is thinking aloud, or there's been a conversation about mothers and fathers and this is halfway through it. Again, it sounds as if he's just chatting to the reader.

Now for another Roald Dahl trick . . . it's one very small word: we. Roald was brilliant at getting readers on his side. By using the word 'we', it's as if he gets the reader to become his friend, or join his gang while he is telling the story. He doesn't really know that 'we' all think that parents who boast about their children make 'us' sick! He just gets us thinking that we do by saying that we do! When writers do this – especially if it's funny – it can feel kind of cosy. Roald Dahl and others also do it with the word 'you'. I could write, 'Hey, you know how when you're ill and you're lying in bed . . .' and, in one stroke, I've sounded as if I know you, you know me and we're all in the same situation – being ill. If you ever watch stand-up comedians, they do exactly the same thing.

Did you realize that Roald Dahl had squeezed so much into the very beginning of *Matilda*? Put all of these fantastic writing techniques and tricks together and they add up to one thing: a great way to grab someone's attention. It certainly worked for me!

Next, let's dive into *James and the Giant Peach* to one of my very favourite parts, at the end of Chapter Five and beginning of Chapter Six:

> *He picked up the chopper and was just about to start chopping away again when he heard a shout behind him that made him stop and turn.*
>
> *'Sponge! Sponge! Come here at once and look at this!'*
> *'At what?'*
> *'It's a peach!' Aunt Spiker was shouting.*
> *'A what?'*
> *'A peach! Right up there on the highest branch! Can't you see it?'*

'I think you must be mistaken, my dear Spiker. That miserable tree never has any peaches on it.'

'There's one on it now, Sponge! You look for yourself!'

'You're teasing me, Spiker. You're making my mouth water on purpose when there's nothing to put into it. Why, that tree's never even had a blossom on it, let alone a peach. Right up on the highest branch, you say? I can't see a thing. Very funny . . . Ha, ha . . . Good gracious me! Well, I'll be blowed! There really is a peach up there!'

'A nice big one, too!' Aunt Spiker said.

'A beauty, a beauty!' Aunt Sponge cried out.

At this point, James slowly put down his chopper and turned and looked across at the two women who were standing underneath the peach tree.

Something is about to happen, he told himself. *Something peculiar is about to happen any moment.*

Here, Roald is building suspense. Writing can be a bit like unfolding something, like a game of pass-the-parcel. Slowly, the writer reveals what's happening. But that's only half of what's going on . . . Writers are very cunning people who are not only unfolding and revealing. Just like conjurors and magicians, they are hiding stuff too. Imagine Roald Dahl sitting in his hut. He knows what's coming next. He knows that he's going to tell you about a peach. He knows that he's going to tell you about a GIANT peach. But as he's writing, he's got to keep that wonderful, top-secret information hidden for as long as he can, while making you desperate to know more.

One way of doing this is to reveal details v-e-r-y slowly, bit by bit. Here, Roald does this through the eyes of someone who doesn't believe in the amazing thing that's happening right before her eyes. Aunt Sponge says, '*I think you must be mistaken.*' We are pretty sure that it's *her* who is mistaken, because we have inside knowledge from earlier in the book. We – the readers or listeners or viewers – know more about what's going on than one or all of the characters. And this sometimes makes us so edgy and involved that we want to SHOUT at the character who doesn't know what's going on, just like the audience does at a pantomime.

Then James tells himself, '*Something is about to happen.*' This takes us into the mind of one of the characters, giving us insider knowledge. And, because we know what James is thinking, it's almost as if he knows that we know! It's also a way of building suspense. By taking time to say that 'something is about to happen', it delays for another moment the very thing that is about to happen! It might make us say to ourselves, 'Go on, go on, happen!' It keeps us hooked.

In the first chapter of *James and the Giant Peach*, this happens:

. . . one day, James's mother and father went to London to do some shopping, and there a terrible thing happened. Both of them suddenly got eaten up (in full daylight, mind you, and on a crowded street) by an enormous angry rhinoceros which had escaped from the London Zoo.

Now this, as you can well imagine, was a rather nasty experience for two such gentle parents.

Is this sad or funny? I think it's funny. But how can Roald Dahl make it sound as if a child losing his parents is funny? He does this in lots of clever ways: he makes the terrible event happen in a flash; he makes it happen in a totally crazy and impossible way (rhinoceroses don't escape from zoos, and even if they did, they would eat grass, not meat); and then he finishes by saying that it was 'a rather nasty experience', when we know that it would really be a sad and tragic thing.

As the story goes on, Roald introduces Aunt Sponge and Aunt Spiker, James's new guardians:

They were selfish and lazy and cruel and right from the beginning they started beating poor James for almost no reason at all. They never called him by his real name, but always referred to him as 'you disgusting little beast' or 'you filthy nuisance' or 'you miserable creature', and they certainly never gave him any toys to play with or any picture books to look at. His room was as bare as a prison cell.

Again, Roald makes an awful thing sound funny. James hasn't done anything wrong and he doesn't deserve any punishment, yet here he is being mistreated. At once, I feel sorry for him and hope that this is going to be a story with a happy ending.

But Roald does something else too: he makes sure we are very firmly on James's side. I think this is one of the most important things about his writing. Over and over again, his readers are on the side of the child against horrible adults. For some adults, this makes his books shocking – even rather nasty. For millions of children, it's made them funny, exciting, naughty and even a bit dangerous.

There's one fairy tale that particularly reminds me of *James and the Giant Peach* and that is *Cinderella*. Just like poor Cinderella, James is stuck with two horrible, ugly sisters. When writers write stories, they can't escape from the stories that have been written before, especially the really famous ones like fairy tales. It's almost as if they're haunted by the old stories, so that when they write the ghost of an old story turns up. This can make us feel that we're at home in the story, rather as if we're in a room and recognize the furniture. But it can also mean that the differences between the old story and the new one give us extra surprises and extra fun. I think Roald Dahl knew that very well.

Roald Dahl specialized in the fantastic and the amazing. Nearly all of his books feature odd, bizarre and weird stuff. He even used the word 'fantastic' in the title of one of his books. (And – ahem – so did I.) These fantastic and amazing storylines often involved incredible schemes and plans. One of my absolute favourites appears in *Danny the Champion of the World*:

. . . My father came in and lit the oil-lamp hanging from the ceiling. It was getting dark earlier now. 'All right,' he said. 'What sort of story shall we have tonight?'

'Dad,' I said. 'Wait a minute.'

'What is it?'

'Can I ask you something? I've just had a bit of an idea.'

'Go on,' he said.

'You know that bottle of sleeping pills Doc Spencer gave you when you came back from hospital?'

'I never used them. Don't like the things.'

'Yes, but is there any reason why those wouldn't work on a pheasant?'

My father shook his head sadly from side to side.

'Wait,' I said.

'It's no use, Danny. No pheasant in the world is going to swallow those lousy red capsules. Surely you know that.'

'You're forgetting the raisins, Dad.'

'The raisins? What's that got to do with it?'

'Now listen,' I said. 'Please listen. We take a raisin. We soak it till it swells. Then we make a tiny slit in one side of it with a razor-blade. Then we hollow it out a little. Then we open up one of your red capsules and pour all the powder into the raisin. Then we get a needle and thread and very carefully we sew up the slit . . .'

Out of the corner of my eye, I saw my father's mouth slowly beginning to open.

Here, Roald is building suspense again. At first, the adult doesn't believe what the child is saying. Then, bit by bit, more details are slowly revealed, while at the same time others are kept hidden – the conjuror's trick again. This time, something is being revealed that will make life better for the characters Roald has made us care about. It's a FANTASTIC plan. It's crazy, wild, weird and maybe even IMPOSSIBLE . . .

But hang on a minute. Maybe it is possible? Wouldn't it be brilliant if it were possible?

If a writer can make a reader really want something to be possible, then I think they've done a brilliant job. And Roald Dahl was an absolute master at doing it. On page after page after page. In book after book after book.

I think that's pretty much all I have to say about him. Or very, very nearly all . . .

Postscript

The last time I saw Roald Dahl was at an event in 1988, when he won the Children's Book Award from the Federation of Children's Book Groups for *Matilda*. I was asked to pop over and say hello to him. He was sitting down next to his wife, Liccy, while various people were asking for his autograph and telling him how much they loved his books. I remember that he looked at me and said – almost as if he was talking to all the children's book writers in the world – 'Well, it's over to you now. You're the ones who've got to do the writing now. I've done my bit . . .'

At the time, I thought that this was an odd thing to say. Surely he wasn't going to stop writing now, just when the whole world seemed to be waiting for whatever he wanted to write next? Well, it wasn't quite the end. Roald did write more. But he was very ill and two years later, in 1990, he died. He was seventy-four.

But, of course, that isn't the end. Anyone and everyone can read Roald Dahl's books, or listen to him and others reading them, or stare goggle-eyed at the many film versions, or watch a real live musical at the theatre!

There's even a Roald Dahl Museum and Story

Centre in Great Missenden, Buckinghamshire. It's a marvellous day out, you can find out all sorts of things to do with Roald Dahl's life, and you can even explore his hut with all its original contents. You can go on a 'trail' and see places round the village that he used in his stories, like an old petrol pump which appears in . . . do you know which story? Belonging to someone's father?

Those who want to find out even more about Roald Dahl can arrange to visit the Museum's archive. It's a special store of his handwritten works – stories, poems, letters, scripts, notebooks and scribbled-down notes. The contents are so precious that they have to be kept in a very large, very dry fridge. I've included some things from the archive in this book – the letters he wrote home to his mother and sisters, and the early storylines for his books.

As I've been writing this book, I've been trying to find out what sort of person Roald Dahl was and asking myself what were the ingredients that made him into such a wonderful writer – the Fantastic Mr Dahl.

I hope I've come up with some answers for you.

Acknowledgements

The author and publisher would like to thank Dahl and Dahl Ltd and the Roald Dahl Museum and Story Centre in Great Missenden, Buckinghamshire, for their kind help and assistance, and the following for permission to use the copyright material below:

Additional illustrations from *More About Boy*, copyright © Quentin Blake and Rowan Clifford, 2008; extracts from *Boy*, text and illustrations copyright © Roald Dahl Nominee Ltd, 1984; *The BFG*, text copyright © Roald Dahl Nominee Ltd, 1982; *Danny the Champion of the World*, text copyright © Roald Dahl Nominee Ltd, 1975; 'First Fig', published in *First Figs from Thistles*, published by Harper & Bros., copyright © The Edna St Vincent Millay Society, 1922; *Going Solo*, text copyright © Roald Dahl Nominee Ltd, 1986; *James and the Giant Peach*, text copyright © Roald Dahl Nominee Ltd, 1961; *Matilda*, text copyright © Roald Dahl Nominee Ltd, 1988; *Roald Dahl's Cookbook* by Felicity and Roald Dahl, text copyright © Roald Dahl Nominee Ltd, 1991.

References: *Storyteller: The Life of Roald Dahl* by Donald Sturrock, first published by HarperCollins Publishers, 2010. *D is for Dahl*, first published by Puffin Books, 2004. *More About Boy: Roald Dahl's Tales from Childhood*, first published by Puffin Books, 2008.

Bibliography

Books by Roald Dahl in chronological order

The Gremlins, first published in the USA by Walt Disney/Random House, 1943

James and the Giant Peach, first published in the USA by Alfred A. Knopf, Inc., 1961; published in Great Britain by George Allen and Unwin, 1967

Charlie and the Chocolate Factory, first published in the USA by Alfred A. Knopf, Inc., 1964; published in Great Britain by George Allen and Unwin, 1967

The Magic Finger, first published in the USA by Harper & Row, 1966; published in Great Britain by George Allen and Unwin, 1968

Fantastic Mr Fox, first published by George Allen and Unwin, 1970

Charlie and the Great Glass Elevator, first published in the USA by Alfred A. Knopf, Inc., 1972; published in Great Britain by George Allen and Unwin, 1973

Danny the Champion of the World, first published by Jonathan Cape, 1975

The Wonderful Story of Henry Sugar and Six More, first published by Jonathan Cape, 1977

The Enormous Crocodile, first published by Jonathan Cape, 1978

The Twits, first published by Jonathan Cape, 1980

George's Marvellous Medicine, first published by Jonathan Cape, 1981

The BFG, first published in Great Britain by Jonathan Cape and in the USA by Farrar, Straus and Giroux, 1982

Revolting Rhymes, first published by Jonathan Cape, 1982

The Witches, first published in Great Britain by Jonathan Cape and in the USA by Farrar, Straus and Giroux, 1983

Dirty Beasts, first published in the USA by Farrar, Straus and Giroux, 1983; published in Great Britain by Jonathan Cape, 1984

Boy: Tales of Childhood, first published in Great Britain by Jonathan Cape and in the USA by Farrar, Straus and Giroux, 1984

The Giraffe and the Pelly and Me, first published in Great Britain by Jonathan Cape and in the USA by Farrar, Straus and Giroux, 1985

Going Solo, first published in Great Britain by Jonathan Cape and in the USA by Farrar, Straus and Giroux, 1986

The Complete Adventures of Charlie and Mr Willy Wonka (a bind-up of *Charlie and the Chocolate Factory* and *Charlie and the Great Glass Elevator*), first published by Unwin Hyman, 1987

Matilda, first published by Jonathan Cape, 1988

Rhyme Stew, first published by Jonathan Cape, 1989

Esio Trot, first published in Great Britain by Jonathan Cape and in the USA by Viking Penguin, 1990

These books were completed before his death in 1990, but published posthumously:

The Minpins, first published by Jonathan Cape, 1991

The Vicar Of Nibbleswicke, first published by Random Century Ltd, 1991

My Year, first published by Jonathan Cape, 1993

These books have been carefully collected together from Roald's papers and previously published material:

The Great Automatic Grammatizator and Other Stories, first published by Viking, 1996

The Roald Dahl Treasury, first published by Jonathan Cape, 1997

Skin and Other Stories, first published by Puffin Books 2000

D is for Dahl, first published by Puffin Books, 2004

Songs and Verse, first published by Jonathan Cape, 2005

More about Boy – this special edition was published with new material by Puffin Books, 2008

Spotty Powder and Other Splendiferous Secrets, first published by Puffin Books, 2008

And some of Roald Dahl's novels have been cleverly adapted into plays:

Charlie and the Chocolate Factory: A Play (adapted by Richard George), first published in the USA by Alfred A. Knopf, Inc., 1976; published in Great Britain by Puffin Books, 1979

James and the Giant Peach: A Play (adapted by Richard George), first published by Puffin Books, 1982

Fantastic Mr Fox: A Play (adapted by Sally Reid), first published by Unwin Hyman and Puffin Books, 1987

The BFG: Plays for Children (adapted by David Wood), first published by Puffin Books, 1993

The Witches: Plays for Children (adapted by David Wood), first published by Puffin Books, 2001

The Twits: Plays for Children (adapted by David Wood), first published by Puffin Books, 2003

Danny the Champion of the World: Plays for Children (adapted by David Wood), first published by Puffin Books, 2009

ROALD DAHL

 1916 Roald Dahl was born on 13 September in Llandaff in Wales.

 1925 Roald was sent to boarding school – St Peter's School in Weston-super-Mare.

 1929 Roald went to Repton, another boarding school. It was here that he helped to test new chocolate bars for Cadbury's. Favourites included Aero, Crunchie, KitKat, Mars and Smarties.

 1934 Roald Dahl left school and went to work for Shell, the big oil company, because he wanted to travel to magical faraway places like Africa and China.

 1936 Shell sent him to east Africa. He hated the snakes!

 1939 Roald Dahl joined the RAF at the start of the Second World War. He became a fighter pilot, flying Hurricane aeroplanes across the Mediterranean Sea.

 1940 His plane crashed in the Western Desert, in north Africa, and he received severe injuries to his head, nose and back.

 1942 Roald was sent to the USA to work in the British Embassy (and some say he was also a spy!). His first adult story was published and he wrote his first story for children, about mischievous creatures called Gremlins. Walt Disney started work on turning it into a film and Roald went to Hollywood.

1943 Movie plans ground to a halt, but *The Gremlins* was published in the USA, Britain and Australia. It was Roald's first book.

 1953 Roald's book of spine-tingling stories for adults, *Someone Like You*, was published and was a huge success in the USA.

1961 *James and the Giant Peach* was published in the USA, followed by *Charlie and the Chocolate Factory* in 1964. It was an instant hit with children.

1967 *James* and *Charlie* were finally published in Britain and have become two of the most successful and popular children's books ever.

1971 The first *Charlie* film was made as *Willy Wonka and the Chocolate Factory*. Other films followed: *The BFG* and *Danny the Champion of the World* in 1989; *The Witches* in 1990; *James and the Giant Peach* and *Matilda* in 1996; the second *Charlie and the Chocolate Factory*, starring Johnny Depp, came out in 2005.

 1978 Roald Dahl's partnership with Quentin Blake began with the publication of *The Enormous Crocodile*.

 1990 Roald Dahl died on 23 November, aged seventy-four.

 2006 and beyond Roald Dahl Day is celebrated all over the world on 13 September to mark Roald Dahl's birthday. Visit **roalddahlday.info** to join the fun.

ROALD DAHL SAYS

'I think probably kindness is my number one attribute in a human being. I'll put it before any of the things like courage or bravery or generosity or anything else. If you're kind, that's it.'

'I am totally convinced that most grown-ups have completely forgotten what it is like to be a child between the ages of five and ten . . . I can remember exactly what it was like. I am certain I can.'

'When I first thought about writing the book *Charlie and the Chocolate Factory*, I never originally meant to have children in it at all!'

'If I had my way, I would remove January from the calendar altogether and have an extra July instead.'

'You can write about anything for children as long as you've got humour.'